www. **Tameside** gov uk

Tamesid
TENANCY

ROGER SPROSTON

STRAIGHTFORWARD PUBLISHING
WWW.STRAIGHTFORWARDCO.CO.UK

Straightforward Publishing

© Straightforward Publishing 2013

ISBN 9781847163684

Printed by Berforts Press

Cover design by Bookworks Islington

The information in this book was correct at the time of going to print. The
author and publishers cannot be held liable for any errors or omissions within
or for any changes in law since publication.

CONTENTS

Introduction

INTRODUCTION

This latest edition of A Straightforward Guide to the Rights of the Private Tenant, substantially updates the previous edition by introducing more detailed information concerning the law, landlords obligations and tenants rights and obligations. It also includes a brief section on leaseholders.

More and more people, in the next few years, due to factors such as changes in the housing benefit system and homelessness legislation will become reliant on the private sector. The private sector is showing signs of rapid expansion and rents are on the increase. In their recent report, Generation Rent, A Society Divided the Halifax states that the private rented sector is now at its highest level since the early 1990'2. In 2011-2012 there were an estimated 22 million households in England and Wales living in private accommodation. With no prospect of buying, more and more people will populate the private market over the coming years. Correspondingly, many more people have become landlords, particularly since 1988, and many more are set to become landlords and it is the case, unfortunately, that this expansion introduces a lot of inexperienced people into the field. If an agent is used in the letting of property then there is (usually) no problem. However, when the property is directly managed then issues can arise that can lead to conflict.

The aim of this book is to ensure that all are clear about the law and practice of letting and residing in, private sector tenanted property.

The book covers the finding of a property, the law, detailed information on specific tenancies, payments of rent and benefits and repairing obligations. Issues such as unlawful eviction and harassment are covered, as are public sector tenancies plus tenancies in Scotland.

There is a section on the processes involved in regaining possession of a home for breach of tenancy.

Finally, although primarily this book is for the private tenant, there is a section for leaseholders of flats, who can be seen as long tenants as a lot of their rights are derived from the Landlord and Tenant Acts, and irresponsible actions by landlords, in particular in relation to service charges, can affect the well being of leaseholders, who are long tenants.

The various notices used when going to court, and other forms associated with landlord and tenant can be obtained from the county courts. The internet site, www.courtservice.org can be accessed and all the necessary forms required in relation to housing matters can be downloaded for free. The court service website also gives a lot of valuable information in relation to housing.

The main aim of this book is to inform the would-be tenant, or the landlord, about their rights and obligations and covers all areas in depth. It is to be hoped that an invaluable insight is gained and that both landlord and tenant can operate more effectively.

Roger Sproston

1

FINDING A PROPERTY

Letting Agents

When looking for a property, there are obvious advantages to using a reputable agent (emphasize reputable): they are likely to be experienced, can provide you with a tenancy agreement and they can provide a service after the property is let. It is important for a tenant to know that there will be a proper relationship between him/her and the landlord after moving in. Managing agents will provide this link.

Agents will typically look after the following:
- Take up references/sign tenancy/take deposit.
- Transfer the utility bills and the council tax into the name of the tenant.
- Pay for repairs, although an agent will only normally do this if rent is being paid directly to them and they can make appropriate deductions.
- Chase rent arrears
- Serve notices of intent to seek possession if the landlord instructs them to do. An agent cannot commence court proceedings except through a solicitor.
- Visit the property at regular intervals and check that the tenants are not causing any damage.
- Deal with neighbor complaints
- Bank rental receipts if the landlord is abroad
- Deal with housing benefit departments if necessary.

The extent to which agents actually do all of the above really depends on the caliber of the agent. It also depends on the type of agreement the landlord has with the agent.

Beware! There are many so-called rental agencies, which have sprung up since the last property recession in the 1990's and also the advent of "Buy to Let". These agents are not professional, do not know a thing about property management, are shady and should be avoided like the plague. Many of them will try to charge an upfront fee, sometimes amounting to £700 (the average is £300) for processing documents. A good lettings agent will charge no fee at all, as they receive fees from landlords when letting the property.

It is most important to shop around and seek a reputable agent. In a climate of shortage of good private rented stock, where there is competition, in places such as London in particular, rogue 'agents' carry out scams such as letting non-existent properties or letting the same property twice. It is very wise to have your wits about you and ensure that you are dealing with honest, reputable agents.

Advertisements

The classified advertisement section of local papers is a good place to seek a property, local papers are obviously cheaper than the nationals such as the Evening Standard in London or the broadsheets such as the Guardian. The type of newspaper you look in will largely reflect what type of property you are looking for. An advert in the pages of the Times would indicate that the landlord is looking for a well-heeled professional and this would be reflected in the type of property that is to let.

Company lets

Where the tenant is a company rather than an individual, the tenancy agreement will be similar to an assured shorthold, but will not be bound by the six-month rule (see chapter 7 for details of assured shorthold tenancies). Company lets can be from any length of time, from a week to several years, or as long as you like. The major difference between contracts and standard assured shorthold agreements is that the contract will be tailored to individual needs, and the agreement is bound by the provisions of contract law. Company tenancies are bound by the provisions of contract law and not by the 1988 Housing Act. Note: if you are a company and you are looking for a property to rent or let you must use a letting agent or solicitor.

The advantages of a landlord letting to a company are:

- A company or embassy has no security of tenure and therefore cannot be a sitting tenant.
- A company cannot seek to reduce the rent by statutory interventions.
- Rental payments are often made quarterly or six monthly in advance.
- The financial status of a company is usually more secure than that of an individual.
- Company tenants often require long-term lets to accommodate staff relocating on contracts of between one and five years.

The main disadvantages of company lets are:

- A company tenancy can only be to a bona fide company or embassy, not to a private individual.

- A tenancy to a partnership would not count as a company let and may have some security of tenure.
- If the tenant is a foreign government, the diplomatic status of the occupant must be ascertained, as the courts cannot enforce breaches of contract with somebody who possesses diplomatic immunity.
- A tenancy to a foreign company not registered in the U.☒ may prove time consuming and costly if it becomes necessary to pursue claims for unpaid rent or damage through foreign courts.

Short lets

Although company lets can be of any length, it is becoming increasingly popular for companies to rent flats from private landlords on short lets.

A short let is any let of less than six months. But here, it is essential to check the rules with any borough concerned. Some boroughs will not allow lets for less than three months, as they do not want to encourage transient people in the neighborhood.

Generally speaking, short lets are only applicable in large cities where there is a substantial shifting population. Business executives on temporary relocation, actors and others involved in television production or film work, contract workers and visiting academics are examples of people who might require a short let.

From a landlord's point of view, short lets are an excellent idea if you have to vacate your own home for seven or eight months, say, and do not want to leave it empty for that time. Short let tenants provide useful extra income as well as keeping an eye on the place.

Short let tenants are, usually, from a landlord's point of view, excellent blue-chip occupants. They are busy professionals, high earners, out all day and used to high standards. As the rent is paid by the company there is no worry for the landlord on this score either.

A major plus of short lets is that they command between 20-50% more rent than the optimum market rent for that type of property. The one downside of short lets is that no agency can guarantee permanent occupancy.

Student lets
Many letting agencies will not consider students and a lot of landlords similarly are not keen. There is the perception that students will not look after a home and tend to live a lifestyle guaranteed to increase the wear and tear on a property. However, if handled correctly, student lets can be profitable.

Although students quite often want property for only eight or nine months, agencies that deal with students make them sign for a whole year. Rent is guaranteed by confirmation that the student is a genuine student with references from parents, who act as guarantors.

Landlords know that there can be a lot of money made from student lets. However, the tenancy will require more avid policing because of the nature of student lifestyle.

If you are a student, you should locate an agency that specializes in student lets or look in the local newspaper which will advertise houses or flats, usually with a room rental rate.

The DSS and housing benefit

Until recently, very few letting agencies or landlords would touch DSS or housing benefit tenants. However, as with student lets, there is another side of the coin. In addition, times are changing and landlords are seeing a new business opportunity with more reliance by local authorities and housing associations, on the private rented sector.

Quite often it is essential for a tenant on HB to have a guarantor, usually a homeowner, before signing a tenancy. Then it is up to the machinations of the benefit system to ensure that the landlord receives rent. The rent is assessed by a benefit officer, with the rent estimated usually at market price. There are rent levels set for each area that the benefit officer will not go above. A deposit is paid normally and rent is paid, in some cases, direct to the landlord. We will be discussing benefits later on in the book.

Holiday lets

Before the Housing Act 1988 became law, many landlords advertised their properties as holiday lets to bypass the rules regarding security of tenure. Strictly speaking, a holiday let is a property let for no more than a month to any one tenant. If the same tenant renews for another month then the landlord is breaking the law. Nowadays, holiday lets must be just that-let for a genuine holiday.

Holiday lets are not covered by the Housing Act. The contract is finalized by exchange of letters with the tenant where they place a deposit and the owner confirms the booking. If the let is not for a genuine holiday you may have problems in evicting the tenant, as the whole point of a holiday let is that it is for no more than a fixed period of a month.

Generally speaking, certain services must be provided for the let to be deemed a holiday let. Cleaning services and changes of bed linen are essential. The amount paid by the holidaymaker will usually include utilities but would exclude use of the telephone, fax machine etc.

If possible, you should talk to someone with some experience of this type of let before entering into an agreement with an agency. The usual problems may arise, those of ensuring occupancy all year round and the maintenance of your property, which will be higher due to a high turnover.

Bedsits

Bedsitting rooms are usually difficult to let and can cause problems for tenants as well as landlords. However, they are usually plentiful, as are studios. Make sure that you have a clear idea of what facilities are available and what the rent includes, i.e. does it include water or council tax.

Viewing a property-The tenant

Once you have found a property, the next stage is to make arrangements for a viewing. It is a good idea to make all appointments on the same day in order to avoid wasting time. If you decide on a likely property, the landlord will wish to take up references, if an agency is not being used. This will normally be a previous landlord's reference and also a bank reference. Only when these have been received and it is established that the person(s) are safe will the letting go ahead. No keys will be handed over until the cheque has been cleared and the landlord is in receipt of a month's rent and a month's deposit.

Deposits

Tenancy Deposit Protection Scheme

The Tenancy Deposit Protection Scheme was introduced to protect all deposits paid to landlords after 6th April 2007. After this date, landlords and/or agents must use a government authorised scheme to protect deposits. The need for such a scheme has arisen because of the historical problem with deposits and the abuse of deposits by landlords. The scheme works as follows:

Moving into a property

At the beginning of a new tenancy agreement, the tenant will pay a deposit to the landlord or agent as usual. Within 14 days the landlord is required to give 30 the tenant details of how the deposit is going to be protected including:

- the contact details of the tenancy deposit scheme
- the contact details of landlord or agent
- how to apply for the release of the deposit
- what to do if there is a dispute about the deposit

There are three tenancy deposit schemes that a landlord can opt for:

Tenancy Deposit Solutions Ltd
www.mydeosits.co.uk
info@mydeposits.co.uk
The Tenancy Deposit Scheme
www.tds.gb.com
0845 226 7837

The Deposit Protection Service
www.depositprotection.com
0870 707 1 707

The schemes above fall into two categories, insurance based schemes and custodial schemes.

Custodial Scheme

- The tenant pays the deposit to the landlord
- The landlord pays the deposit into the scheme
- Within 14 days of receiving the deposit, the landlord must give the tenant prescribed information
- A the end of the tenancy, if the landlord and tenant have agreed how much of the deposit is to be returned, they will tell the scheme which returns the deposit, divided in the way agreed by the parties.
- If there is a dispute, the scheme will hold the disputed amount until the dispute resolution service or courts decide what is fair
- The interest accrued by deposits in the scheme will be used to pay for the running of the scheme and any surplus will be used to offer interest to the tenant, or landlord if the tenant isn't entitled to it.

Insurance based schemes

- The tenant pays the deposit to the landlord
- The landlord retains the deposit and pays a premium to the insurer (this is the key difference between the two schemes)

- Within 14 days of receiving a deposit the landlord must give the tenant prescribed information.
- At the end of the tenancy if the landlord and tenant agree how the deposit is to be divided or otherwise then the landlord will return the amount agreed
- If there is a dispute, the landlord must hand over the disputed amount to the scheme for safekeeping until the dispute is resolved
- If for any reason the landlord fails to comply, the insurance arrangements will ensure the return of the deposit to the tenant if they are entitled to it.

If a landlord or agent hasn't protected a deposit with one of the above then the tenant can apply to the local county court for an order for the landlord either to protect the deposit or repay it.

Rental guarantees

The landlord will always obtain a guarantor if there is any potential uncertainty as to payment of rent. One example is where the tenant is on benefits. The guarantor will be expected to assume responsibility for the rent if the tenant ceases to pay at any time during the term of the tenancy.

In chapter two we will explore the legal framework governing residential lettings.

2

THE LAW IN A NUTSHELL

Explaining the law

As a tenant, or potential tenant, it is very important to understand the rights and obligations of both yourself and your landlord, exactly what can and what cannot be done once the tenancy agreement has been signed and you have moved into the property.

Some landlords think they can do exactly as they please, because the property belongs to them. Some tenants do not know any differently and therefore the landlord can, and often does, get away with breaking the law. However there is a very strong legal framework governing the relationship between landlord and tenant and it is important that you have a grasp of the key principles of the law.

In order to fully understand the law we should begin by looking at the main types of relationship between people and their homes.

The freehold and the lease

In law, there are two main types of ownership and occupation of property. These are: freehold and leasehold. These arrangements are very old indeed. In the section dealing with the relationship between leaseholder and freeholder, towards the end of this book, we will be discussing leasehold and freehold in more depth.

Freehold

If a person owns their property outright (usually with a mortgage) then they are a freeholder. The only claims to ownership over and above their own might be those of the building society or the bank, which lent them the money to buy the property. They will re-possess the property if the mortgage payments are not kept up with.

In certain situations though, the local authority (council) for an area can affect a person's right to do what they please with their home even if they are a freeholder. This will occur when planning powers are exercised, for example, in order to prevent the carrying out of alterations without consent.

The local authority for your area has many powers and we will be referring to these regularly.

Leasehold

If a person lives in a property owned by someone else and has a written agreement allowing them to occupy the flat or house for a period of time i.e., giving them permission to live in that property, then they will, in the main, have a lease and either be a leaseholder or a tenant of a landlord.

The main principle of a lease is that a person has been given permission by someone else to live in his or her property for a period of time. The person giving permission could be either the freeholder or another leaseholder. The tenancy agreement is one type of lease. If you have signed a tenancy agreement then you will have been given permission by a person to live in their property for a period of time.

The position of the tenant

The tenant will usually have an agreement for a shorter period of time than the typical leaseholder. Whereas the leaseholder will, for example, have an agreement for ninety-nine years, the tenant will have an agreement, which either runs from week to week or month to month (periodic tenancy) or is for a fixed term, for example, six-months or one-year.

These arrangements are the most common types of agreement between the private landlord and tenant.

The agreement itself will state whether it is a fixed term or periodic tenancy. If an agreement has not been issued it will be assumed to be a fixed-term tenancy.

Both periodic and fixed term tenants will usually pay a sum of rent regularly to a landlord in return for permission to live in the property (more about rent and service charges later)

The tenancy agreement

The tenancy agreement is the usual arrangement under which one person will live in a property owned by another. Before a tenant moves into a property he/she will have to sign a tenancy agreement drawn up by a landlord or landlord's agent. *A tenancy agreement is a contract between landlord and tenant.*

It is important to realize that when you sign a tenancy agreement, you have signed a contract with another person, which governs the way in which you will live in their property.

The contract

Typically, any tenancy agreement will show the name and address of the landlord and will state the names of the tenant(s). The type of tenancy agreement that is signed should be clearly indicated. This could be, for example, a Rent Act protected tenancy, an assured tenancy or an assured shorthold tenancy. In the main, in the private sector, the agreement will be an assured shorthold.

Date of commencement of tenancy and rent payable

The date the tenancy began and the duration (fixed term or periodic) plus the amount of rent payable should be clearly shown, along with who is responsible for any other charges, such as water rates, council tax etc, and a description of the property you are living in.

In addition to the rent that must be paid there should be a clear indication of when a rent increase can be expected. This information is sometimes shown in other conditions of tenancy, which should be given to the tenant when they move into their home. The conditions of tenancy will set out landlords and tenants rights and obligations.

Services provided under the tenancy and service of notice

If services are provided, i.e., if a service charge is payable, this should be indicated in the agreement. The tenancy agreement should indicate clearly the address to which notices on the landlord can be served by the tenant, for example, because of repair problems or notice of leaving the property. The landlord has a legal requirement to indicate this.

Tenants obligations

The tenancy agreement will either be a basic document with the above information or will be more comprehensive. Either way, there will be a section beginning "the tenant agrees." Here the tenant will agree to move into the property, pay rent, use the property as an only home, not cause a nuisance to others, take responsibility for certain internal repairs, not sublet the property, i.e., create another tenancy, and various other things depending on the property.

24

Landlords obligations

There should also be another section "the landlord agrees". Here, the landlord is contracting with the tenant to allow quiet enjoyment of the property. The landlord's repairing responsibilities are also usually outlined.

Ending a tenancy

Finally, there should be a section entitled "ending the tenancy" which will outline the ways in which landlord and tenant can end the agreement. The landlord can only end a fixed term assured shorthold tenancy by issuing a s21 notice (so called because it arises out of section 21 of the Housing Act 1988, as amended) two months prior to the end of the tenancy. Many landlords issue this notice at the outset of the tenancy. The tenant, after the expiry of the fixed term, can give one months notice to leave.

It is also in this section that the landlord should make reference to the "grounds for possession". Grounds for possession are circumstances where the landlord will apply to court for possession of his/her property. Some of these grounds relate to what is in the tenancy, i.e., the responsibility to pay rent and to not cause a nuisance.

Other grounds do not relate to the contents of the tenancy directly, but more to the law governing that particular tenancy. The grounds for possession are very important, as they are used in any court case brought against the tenant. Unfortunately, they are not always indicated in the tenancy agreement. As they are so important they are summarized later on in the next chapter.

It must be said at this point that many residential tenancies are very light on spelling out landlord's responsibilities. For example, repairing responsibilities are landlords obligations under law. This book deals with these obligations, and also other important areas. However, many landlords will seek to use only the most basic document in order to conceal legal obligations.

This is one of the main reasons for this book. It is essential that those who intend to let property for profit are able to manage professionally and set high standards as a private landlord. This is because the sector has been beset by rogues in the past. Correspondingly, as a tenant you need to know your rights very clearly and need to know how to enforce them.

The responsibility of the landlord to provide a tenant with a rent book

If the tenant is a weekly periodic tenant the landlord must provide him/her with a rent book and commits a criminal offence if he/she does not do so. This is outlined in the Landlord and Tenant Act 1985 sections 4 - 7. Under this Act any tenant can ask in writing the name and address of the landlord. The landlord must reply within twenty-one days of asking. As most tenancies nowadays are fixed term assured shortholds then it is not strictly necessary to provide a tenant with a rent book.. However, for the purposes of efficiency, and your own records, it is always useful to have a rent book and sign it each time rent is collected or a standing order is paid.

Overcrowding and the rules governing too many people living in the property

It is important to understand, when signing a tenancy agreement, that it is not permitted to allow the premises to become overcrowded, i.e., to allow more people than was originally intended, (which is outlined in the agreement) to live in the property. If a tenant does, then the landlord can take action to evict.

Different types of tenancy agreement
The protected tenancy - the meaning of the term

As a basic guide, if a person is a private tenant and signed their current agreement with a landlord before 15th January 1989 then they will, in most cases, be a protected tenant with all the rights relating to protection of tenure, which are considerable. Protection is provided under the 1977 Rent Act.

In practice, there are not many protected tenancies left and the tenant will usually be signing an assured shorthold tenancy. Nevertheless, we will be looking briefly at the Protected tenancy in the next chapter.

The assured shorthold tenancy - what it means

If the tenant entered into an agreement with a landlord after 15th January 1989 then they will, in most cases, be an assured tenant. We will discuss assured tenancies in more depth in chapter three. In brief, there are various types of assured tenancy. The assured shorthold is usually a fixed term version of the assured tenancy and enables the landlord to recover their property after six months and to vary the rent after this time. *It is this tenancy that a private tenant will be signing.*

Other types of agreement

In addition to the above tenancy agreements, there are other types of agreement sometimes used in privately rented property. One of these is the company let, as we discussed in the last chapter, and another is the

27

license agreement. The person signing such an agreement is called a licensee. Licenses will only apply in special circumstances where the licensee cannot be given sole occupation of his home and therefore can only stay for a short period with minimum rights.

****

3

MORE ABOUT ASSURED TENANTS

The assured tenant

As we discussed in Chapter two, all tenancies, (with the exceptions detailed entered into after 15th January 1989), are known as assured tenancies. An assured shorthold, which is the most common form of tenancy used by the landlord nowadays, is one type of assured tenancy, and is for a fixed term of six months minimum and can be brought to an end with two months notice by serving a section 21 (of the Housing Act 1988) notice.

It is important to note that all tenancies signed after February 1997 are assured shorthold agreements unless otherwise stated.

Assured tenancies are governed by the 1988 Housing Act, as amended by the 1996 Housing Act. It is to these Acts, or outlines of the Acts that the tenant must refer when intending to sign a tenancy for a residential property.

For a tenancy to be assured, three conditions must be fulfilled:

1. The premises must be a dwelling house. This basically means any premises which can be lived in. Business premises will normally fall outside this interpretation.
2. There must exist a particular relationship between landlord and tenant. In other words there must exist a tenancy agreement. For

example, a license to occupy, as in the case of students, or accommodation occupied as a result of work, cannot be seen as a tenancy. Following on from this, the accommodation must be let as a single unit. The tenant, who must be an individual, must normally be able to sleep, cook and eat in the accommodation. Sharing of bathroom facilities will not prevent a tenancy being an assured tenancy but shared cooking or other facilities, such as a living room, will.

3. The third requirement for an assured tenancy is that the tenant must occupy the dwelling as his or her only or principal home. In situations involving joint tenants at least one of them must occupy.

Tenancies that are not assured

A tenancy agreement will not be assured if one of the following conditions applies:

-The tenancy or the contract was entered into before 15th January 1989;

-If no rent is payable or if only a low rent amounting to less than two thirds of the present ratable value of the property is payable;

-If the premises are let for business purposes or for mixed residential and business purposes;

-If part of the dwelling house is licensed for the sale of liquor for consumption on the premises. This does not include the publican who lets out a flat;

-If the dwelling house is let with more than two acres of agricultural land;

-If the dwelling house is part of an agricultural holding and is occupied in relation to carrying out work on the holding;

-If the premises are let by a specified institution to students, i.e., halls of residence;

-If the premises are let for the purpose of a holiday;

-Where there is a resident landlord, e.g., in the case where the landlord has let one of his rooms but continues to live in the house;

-If the landlord is the Crown (the monarchy) or a government department. Certain lettings by the Crown are capable of being assured, such as some lettings by the Crown Estate Commissioners;

-If the landlord is a local authority, a fully mutual housing association (this is where you have to be a shareholder to be a tenant) a newly created Housing Action Trust or any similar body listed in the 1988 Housing Act.

-If the letting is transitional such as a tenancy continuing in its original form until phased out, such as:

-A protected tenancy under the 1977 Rent Act;
-Secure tenancy granted before 1st January 1989, e.g., from a local authority or housing association. These tenancies are governed by the 1985 Housing Act).

The Assured Shorthold tenancy
The assured shorthold tenancy as we have seen, is the most common

form of tenancy used in the private sector. The main principle of the assured shorthold tenancy is that it is issued for a period of six months minimum and can be brought to an end by the landlord serving two months notice on the tenant. At the end of the six-month period the tenant, if given two months prior notice, must leave. If the tenant refuses to leave then the landlord can use a special 'fast track' procedure to get him/her out.

Any property let on an assured tenancy can be let on an assured shorthold, providing the following three conditions are met:

- The tenancy must be for a fixed term of not less than six months.
- The agreement cannot contain powers which enable the landlord to end the tenancy before six months. This does not include the right of the landlord to enforce the grounds for possession, which will be approximately the same as those for the assured tenancy (see below).
- A notice requiring possession at the end of the term is usually served two months before that date.
- A notice must be served before any rent increase giving one months clear notice and providing details of the rent increase.

If the landlord wishes to get possession of his/her property, in this case before the expiry of the contractual term, the landlord has to gain a court order. A notice of seeking possession must be served, giving fourteen days notice and following similar grounds of possession as an assured tenancy. *The landlord cannot simply tell a tenant to leave before the end of the agreed term.*

If the tenancy runs on after the end of the fixed term then the landlord can regain possession by giving the required two months notice, as mentioned above.

At the end of the term for which the assured shorthold tenancy has been granted, the landlord has an automatic right to possession. An assured shorthold tenancy will become periodic (will run from week to week) when the initial term of six months has elapsed and the landlord has not brought the tenancy to an end. A periodic tenancy is brought to an end with two months notice.

Assured shorthold tenants, can be evicted only on certain grounds some discretionary, some mandatory (see below).

In order for the landlord of an assured shorthold tenant to regain possession of the property, other than issuing a s21 notice, a notice of seeking possession (of property) must be served, giving fourteen days notice of expiry and stating the ground for possession. This notice is similar to a notice to quit, discussed in the previous chapter. Following the fourteen days a court order must be obtained. Although gaining a court order is not complicated, a solicitor will usually be used. Court costs can be awarded against the tenant.

Security of tenure: The ways in which a tenant can lose their home as an assured shorthold tenant

There are a number of circumstances called grounds (mandatory and discretionary) whereby a landlord can start a court action to evict a tenant. The following are the *mandatory* grounds (where the judge must give the landlord possession) and *discretionary* grounds (where the judge does not have to give the landlord possession) on which a court can order possession if the home is subject to an assured tenancy.

The mandatory grounds for possession of a property let on an assured (shorthold) tenancy

There are eight mandatory grounds for possession, which, if proved, leave the court with no choice but to make an order for possession. It is very important that you understand these.

Ground One is used where the landlord has served a notice, no later than at the beginning of the tenancy, warning the tenant that this ground may be used against him/her.

This ground is used where the landlord wishes to recover the property as his or her principal (first and only) home or the spouse's (wife's or husbands) principal home. ***The ground is not available to a person who bought the premises for gain (profit) whilst they were occupied.***

Ground Two is available where the property is subject to a mortgage and if the landlord does not pay the mortgage, could lose the home.

Grounds Three and Four relate to holiday lettings.

Ground Five is a special one, applicable to ministers of religion.

Ground Six relates to the demolition or reconstruction of the property.

Ground Seven applies if a tenant dies and in his will leaves the tenancy to someone else: but the landlord must start proceedings against the new tenant within a year of the death if he wants to evict the new tenant.

Ground Eight concerns rent arrears. This ground applies if, both at the date of the serving of the notice seeking possession and at the date of the hearing of the action, the rent is at least 8 weeks in arrears. This is the main ground used by landlords when rent is not being paid. The landlord should understand that in order to get a court order for possession of property for rent arrears then, because of the short-term nature of the Assured shorthold, time is of the essence. If the tenancy is into the third month, it may be easier to wait and serve a two-month notice of termination and get a court order against the occupants separately.

One of the advantages of a court order is that you will have details of the tenant's employers and can get an attachment of earnings against the tenant.

The discretionary grounds for possession of a property, which is let on an assured tenancy

As we have seen, the discretionary grounds for possession are those in relation to which the court has some powers over whether or not the landlord can evict. In other words, the final decision is left to the judge. Often the judge will prefer to grant a suspended order first, unless the circumstances are dramatic.

Ground Nine applies when suitable alternative accommodation is available or will be when the possession order takes effect. As we have seen, if the landlord wishes to obtain possession of his or her property in order to use it for other purposes then suitable alternative accommodation has to be provided.

Ground Ten deals with rent arrears as does *ground eleven*. These grounds are distinct from the mandatory grounds, as there does not have to be a fixed arrear in terms of time scale, e.g., 8 weeks. The judge, therefore, has some choice as to whether or not to evict. In practice, this ground will not be relevant to managers of assured shorthold tenancies.

Ground Twelve concerns any broken obligation of the tenancy. As we have seen with the protected tenancy, there are a number of conditions of the tenancy agreement, such as the requirement not to racially or sexually harass a neighbor. Ground Twelve will be used if these conditions are broken.

Ground Thirteen deals with the deterioration of the dwelling as a result of a tenant's neglect. This is connected with the structure of the property and is the same as for a protected tenancy. It puts the responsibility on the tenant to look after the premises.

Ground Fourteen concerns nuisance, annoyance and illegal or immoral use. This is where a tenant or anyone connected with the tenant has caused a nuisance to neighbors.

Ground 14A this ground deals with domestic violence.

Ground 15 concerns the condition of the furniture and tenants neglect. As Ground thirteen puts some responsibility on the tenant to look after the structure of the building so Ground Fifteen makes the tenant responsible for the furniture and fittings.

Ground 16 covers former employees. The premises were let to a former tenant by a landlord seeking possession and the tenant has ceased to be in that employment.

Ground 17 is where a person or that persons agents makes a false or reckless statement and this has caused the landlord to grant the tenancy under false pretences.

The description of the grounds above is intended as a guide only. For a fuller description please refer to the 1988 Housing Act, section 7, Schedule two,) as amended by the 1996 Housing Act) which is available at reference libraries.

Fast track possession

In November 1993, following changes to the County Court Rules, a facility was introduced which enabled landlords of tenants with assured shorthold tenancies to apply for possession of their property without the usual time delay involved in waiting for a court date and attendance at court. This is known as "fast track possession" It cannot be used for rent arrears or other grounds. It is used to gain possession of a property when the fixed term of six months or more has come to an end and the tenant will not move. The appropriate forms and fees guidance, plus general guidance on filling the forms and sending them to court can be obtained from the court service website www. hmcourts-service.gov.uk

****

4

JOINT TENANCIES

Joint tenancies: the position of two or more people who have a tenancy agreement for one property. Although it is the normal state of affairs for a tenancy agreement, to be granted to one person, this is not always the case. A tenancy can also be granted to two or more people and is then known as a *joint tenancy*. The position of joint tenants is exactly the same as that of single tenants. In other words, there is still one tenancy even though it is shared

Each tenant is responsible for paying the rent and observing the terms and conditions of the tenancy agreement. No one joint tenant can prevent another joint tenant access to the premises.

If one of the joint tenants dies then his or her interest will automatically pass to the remaining joint tenants. A joint tenant cannot dispose of his or her interest in a will.

If one joint tenant, however, serves a notice to quit (notice to leave the property) on another joint tenant(s) then the tenancy will come to an end and the landlord can apply to court for a possession order, if the remaining tenant does not leave.

The position of a wife or husband in relation to joint tenancies is rather more complex because the married person has more rights when it comes to the home than the single person.

Remember: the position of a tenant who has signed a joint tenancy agreement is exactly the same as that of the single tenant. If one person leaves, the other(s) have the responsibilities of the tenancy. If one person leaves without paying his share of the rent then the other tenants will have to pay instead.

5

RENT AND OTHER CHARGES

The payment of rent and other financial matters

If a tenancy is protected under the Rent Act 1977, as described earlier there is the right to apply to the Rent Officer for the setting of a fair rent for the property. However, as described earlier, the incidence of Rent Act Protected Tenancies has diminished to almost zero.

The assured tenant

The assured tenant has far fewer rights in relation to rent control than the protected tenant. The Housing Act 1988 allows a landlord to charge whatever he likes. There is no right to a fair or reasonable rent with an assured tenancy. If the tenancy is assured then there will usually be a formula in the tenancy which will provide guidance for rent increases. If not then the landlord can set what rent he or she likes within reason. If the amount is unreasonable then the tenant can refer the matter to the local Rent Assessment Committee. The rent can sometimes be negotiated at the outset of the tenancy. This rent has to be paid as long as the contractual term of the tenancy lasts. Once the contractual term has expired, the landlord is entitled to continue to charge the same rent.

On expiry of an assured shorthold the landlord is free to grant a new tenancy and set the rent to a level that is compatible with the market. Details of the local Rent Assessment Committee can be obtained from the Rent Officer Service at your local authority.

Housing Benefit

Housing benefit is a benefit for people on low income to help them pay their rent. You may be able to get housing benefit if you are on other benefits or work part time or full time on a low income.

To get housing benefit in the first place you must pay rent. It doesn't matter who the landlord is, whether private or public sector. You can also claim housing benefit if you rent a room in a hostel or are a boarder. You can claim it if you share a house or flat as point or sub-tenants. You cannot get housing benefit if you rent your home from the Crown, or you are 16 or 17 or have been in care.

Only one member of a couple who live together can claim housing benefit. You must also live in the accommodation for which you are claiming benefit.

Students may be able to claim housing benefit, but special rules will apply.

UK Resident

You must be living in the UK to claim housing benefit. If you are from overseas or have recently arrived in the UK you may have difficulty claiming housing benefit.

Income and capital

To get housing benefit you must have income and capital below a certain level. Capital means savings, land, property or anything else that could provide you with an income. If you have more than £16,000 in capital you will not get housing benefit, unless you are getting the guarantee part of pension credit. If you have capital of over £6,000 you will be assumed to have some income from that capital. f you are getting income support or income based jobseekers allowance, you will automatically be within the income and capital limits for housing benefits. If you are in pension credit and get the guarantee credit (whether on its own or with the savings credit) you will also automatically get the maximum housing benefit amount.

How much benefit can you get?

How much benefit you will get depends on how much rent you pay, what income you have and where you live. The rules for HB allowance are changing which are outlined below. If you pay rent to a private landlord, the rent your housing benefit will cover will normally be restricted to an amount set by the rent officer. When you make a new claim for housing benefit your local authority will normally calculate how much rent your housing benefit can cover suing the Local Authority Housing Allowance Rules. In many cases, however, the amount of HB that you are entitled to will not cover the full amount and you will have to make up the shortfall. There are different rules concerning applications for HB before and after 7th April 2008 and these rules can be obtained from the local authority.

There will be a limit on payments so that the Local Housing Allowance does not exceed:

- £250 per week for a one bedroom property (including shared accommodation)
- £290 a week for a two bedroom property
- £340 a week for a three bedroom property
- £400 a week for a four bedroom property

The maximum rate of HB will be limited to a four-bedroom property. There will be help for disabled people towards the cost of an extra bedroom if they need an overnight carer. Housing benefit is included in the overall cap on benefits that single people and couples can receive.

Shared room rate

This applies to single people under the age of 35 living in accommodation that they rent from a private landlord. Housing benefit is restricted to the average that a single person would pay for a shared house in an area. Previously, the rule applied to those under 25.There are exemptions: single 25-34 year olds who have lived in a homeless hostel for more than three months will still be entitled to a one bed flat, a single 25-34 year old ex-offender who is managed under Multi-Agency Public Protection Arrangements (MAPPA) is exempt and will not be expected to live in shared accommodation. In addition, a person under 22 who has been in care and receives Disability Living Allowance at the medium or higher rate for a severe disability will be exempt.

The above outline of housing benefit is very brief. The local authority in your area will be able to furnish you with full details.

Council tax and the tenant

Council tax is based on properties, or dwellings, and not individual people. This means that there is one bill for each individual dwelling, rather than separate bills for each person. The number and type of people who live in the dwelling may affect the size of the final bill. A discount of 25% is given for people who live alone. Each property is placed in a valuation band with different properties paying more or less depending on their individual value. Tenants who feel that their home has been placed in the wrong valuation band can appeal to their local authority council tax department.

Who has to pay the council tax?

In most cases the tenant occupying the dwelling will have to pay the council tax. However, a landlord will be responsible for paying the council tax where there are several households living in one dwelling. This will usually be hostels, bedsits and other non-self contained flats where people share things such as cooking and washing facilities. The council tax on this type of property remains the responsibility of the landlord even if all but one of the tenants move out. Although the landlord has the responsibility for paying the council tax, he/she will normally try to pass on the increased cost through rents. However, as we have seen, there is a set procedure for a landlord to follow if he/she wishes to increase rent.

Council tax benefits available for those on low income

Tenants on very low income, except for students, will usually be able to claim a council tax reduction. This used to cover up to 100% of the council tax. However, with the widespread changes to benefits in 2013, council tax benefit has now been abolished (after April 2013) and each local authority will be responsible for payment of council tax reduction to individual tenants. Invariably, this will not be 100% so tenants will now be left with a shortfall that they will have to meet.

Tenants with disabilities may be entitled to further discounts. Tenants who are not responsible for individual council tax, but pay it through their rent, can claim housing benefit to cover the increase.

The rules covering council tax liability can be obtained from a Citizens Advice Bureau or from your local authority council tax department.

6

THE RIGHT TO QUIET ENJOYMENT OF A HOME

Earlier, we saw that when a tenancy agreement is signed, the landlord is contracting to give quiet enjoyment of the tenants home. This means that they have the right to live peacefully in the home without harassment.

The landlord is obliged not to do anything that will disturb the right to the quiet enjoyment of the home. The most serious breach of this right would be for the landlord to wrongfully evict a tenant.

Eviction: what can be done against unlawful harassment and eviction

It is a criminal offence for a landlord unlawfully to evict a residential occupier (whether or not a tenant!). The occupier has protection under the Protection from Eviction Act 1977 section 1(2). If the tenant or occupier is unlawfully evicted his/her first course should be to seek an injunction compelling the landlord to readmit him/her to the premises. It is an unfortunate fact but many landlords will attempt to evict tenants forcefully. In doing so they break the law.

However, the landlord may, on termination of the tenancy, recover possession without a court order if the agreement was entered into after 15th January 1989 and it falls into one of the following six situations:

- The occupier shares any accommodation with the landlord and the landlord occupies the premises as his or her only or principal home.
- The occupier shares any of the accommodation with a member of the landlords family, that person occupies the premises as their only or principal home, and the landlord occupies as his or her only or principal home premises in the same building.
- The tenancy or license was granted temporarily to an occupier who entered the premises as a trespasser.
- The tenancy or license gives the right to occupy for the purposes of a holiday.
- The tenancy or license is rent-free.
- The license relates to occupation of a hostel.

There is also a section in the 1977 Protection from Eviction Act which provides a defense for otherwise unlawful eviction and that is that the landlord may repossess if it is thought that the tenant no longer lives on the premises. It is important to note that, in order for such action to be seen as a crime under the 1977 Protection from Eviction Act, the intention of the landlord to evict must be proved.

However, there is another offence, namely harassment, which also needs to be proved. Even if the landlord is not guilty of permanently depriving a tenant of their home he/she could be guilty of harassment. Such actions as cutting off services, deliberately allowing the premises to fall into a state of disrepair, or even forcing unwanted sexual attentions, all constitute harassment and a breach of the right to *quiet enjoyment.*

The 1977 Protection from Eviction Act also prohibits the use of violence to gain entry to premises. Even in situations where the landlord has the right to gain entry without a court order it is an offence to use violence.

What can be done against unlawful evictions?

There are two main remedies for unlawful eviction: damages and, as stated above, an injunction.

The injunction

An injunction is an order from the court requiring a person to do, or not to do something. In the case of eviction the court can grant an injunction requiring the landlord to allow a tenant back into occupation of the premises. In the case of harassment an order can be made preventing the landlord from harassing the tenant. Failure to comply with an injunction is contempt of court and can result in a fine or imprisonment.

Damages

In some cases the tenant can press for *financial compensation* following unlawful eviction. Financial compensation may have to be paid in cases where financial loss has occurred or in cases where personal hardship alone has occurred. The tenant can also press for *special damages,* which means that the tenant may recover the definable out-of-pocket expenses. These could be expenses arising as a result of having to stay in a hotel because of the eviction. Receipts must be kept in that case. There are also *general damages,* which can be awarded in compensation for stress, suffering and inconvenience.

A tenant may also seek *exemplary damages* where it can be proved that the landlord has disregarded the law deliberately with the intention of making a profit out of the displacement of the tenant.

7

REPAIRS-LANDLORDS/TENANTS
OBLIGATIONS

Repairs and improvements generally: The landlord and tenants obligations

Repairs are essential works to keep the property in good order. Improvements and alterations to the property, e.g. the installation of a shower.

As we have seen, most tenancies are periodic, i.e. week-to-week or month-to-month. If a tenancy falls into this category, or is a fixed-term tenancy for less than seven years, and began after October 1961, then a landlord is legally responsible for most major repairs to the flat or house.

If a tenancy began after 15th January 1989 then, in addition to the above responsibility, the landlord is also responsible for repairs to common parts and service fittings.

The area of law dealing with the landlord and tenants repairing obligations is the 1985 Landlord and Tenant Act, section 11.

This section of the Act is known as a covenant and cannot be excluded by informal agreement between landlord and tenant. In other words the landlord is legally responsible whether he or she likes it or not. Parties to a tenancy, however, may make an application to a court mutually to vary or exclude this section.

Example of repairs a landlord is responsible for:

- Leaking roofs and guttering.
- Rotting windows.
- Rising damp.
- Damp walls.
- Faulty electrical wiring.
- Dangerous ceilings and staircases.
- Faulty gas and water pipes.
- Broken water heaters and boilers.
- Broken lavatories, sinks or baths.

In shared housing the landlord must see that shared halls, stairways, kitchens and bathrooms are maintained and kept clean and lit.

Normally, tenants are responsible only for minor repairs, e.g., broken door handles, cupboard doors, etc. Tenants will also be responsible for decorations unless they have been damaged as a result of the landlord's failure to do repair.

A landlord will be responsible for repairs only if the repair has been reported. It is therefore important to report repairs in writing and keep a copy. If the repair is not carried out then action can be taken. Damages can also be claimed.

Compensation can be claimed, with the appropriate amount being the reduction in the value of the premises to the tenant caused by the landlord's failure to repair. If the tenant carries out the repairs then the amount expended will represent the decrease in value.

The tenant does not have the right to withhold rent because of a breach of repairing covenant by the landlord. However, depending on the repair, the landlord will not have a very strong case in court if rent is withheld.

Reporting repairs to landlords

The tenant has to tell the landlord or the person collecting the rent straight away when a repair needs doing. It is advisable that it is in writing, listing the repairs that need to be done.

Once a tenant has reported a repair the landlord must do it within a reasonable period of time. What is reasonable will depend on the nature of the repair. If certain emergency work needs to be done by the council, such as leaking guttering or drains a notice can be served ordering the landlord to do the work within a short time. In exceptional cases if a home cannot be made habitable at reasonable cost the council may declare that the house must no longer be used, in which case the council has a legal duty to re-house a tenant.

If after the council has served notice the landlord still does not do the work, the council can send in its own builder or, in some cases take the landlord to court. A tenant must allow a landlord access to do repairs. The landlord has to give twenty-four hours notice of wishing to gain access.

The tenants rights whilst repairs are being carried out

The landlord must ensure that the repairs are done in an orderly and efficient way with minimum inconvenience to the tenant. If the works are disruptive or if property or decorations are damaged the tenant can apply to the court for compensation or, if necessary, for an order to make the landlord behave reasonably.

If the landlord genuinely needs the house empty to do the work he/she can ask the tenant to vacate it and can if necessary get a court order against the tenant.

A written agreement should be drawn up making it clear that the tenant can move back in when the repairs are completed and stating what the arrangements for fuel charges and rent are.

If a person is an assured tenant the landlord could get a court order to make that person give up the home permanently if there is work to be done with him/her in occupation.

Can the landlord put the rent up after doing repairs?

If there is a service charge for maintenance, the landlord may be able to pass on the cost of the work(s).

Tenants rights to make improvements to a property

Unlike carrying out repairs the tenant will not normally have the right to insist that the landlord make actual alterations to the home. However, a tenant needs the following amenities and the law states that you should have:

- Bath or shower.

- Wash hand basin.
- Hot and cold water at each bath, basin or shower.
- An indoor toilet.

If these amenities do not exist then the tenant can contact the council's Environmental Health Officer. An improvement notice can be served on the landlord ordering him to put the amenity in.

Disabled tenants

If a tenant is disabled he/she may need special items of equipment in the accommodation. The local authority may help in providing and, occasionally, paying for these. The tenant will need to obtain the permission of the landlord. If you require more information then contact the social services department locally.

The Equality Act 2010

The Equality Act 2010 has introduced a new duty on landlords (from October 2010) to consent to changes in common parts of residential or mixed-use buildings in England, Wales and Scotland. This means that if a disabled tenant or occupier who uses or intends to use premises in a building as his or her main home requests physical changes to common parts to reduce or avoid a disadvantage suffered in comparison with non-disabled people, the landlord must within a reasonable time consult all other likely to be affected by the changes and, having considered the views of those consulted, take whatever steps are reasonable to avoid the disadvantage. If changes to the common parts are considered reasonable the landlord must first enter into a written agreement that the disabled person organizes and pays for the work and for restoration of the common parts when the disabled person leaves the property.

The agreement will bind the landlord's successors but not the disabled person's successors. So the landlord may wish to insist that the works are reinstated before the disabled person leaves.

Shared housing. The position of tenants in shared houses (Houses in Multiple Occupation)

A major change to improve standards of shared housing was introduced in 2006. The parts of the Housing Act 2004 relating to the licensing of HMO's (Houses in Multiple Occupation) and the new Health and Safety Rating System for assessing property conditions came into effect on 6rh April 2006. The Act requires landlords of many HMO's to apply for licences. The HMO's that need to be licensed are those with:

- Three or more storeys, which are
- Occupied by five or more people forming two or more households (i.e. people not related, living together as a couple etc) and
- Which have an element of shared facilities (eg kitchen, bathroom etc)

As far as licensing is concerned, attics and basements are included as storeys if they are used as living accommodation. Previously, HMO's were only defined as houses converted into flats or bedsits, but the new Act widens this definition and many more types of shared houses are now included.

A local authority will have a list of designated properties will have a list of those properties which are designated HMO's and they will need to be licensed.

Usually, landlords will need to apply to a local authority private sector unit for licences. It has been illegal for landlords to manage designated properties without a licence since July 2006.

Landlords will have to complete an application form and pay a fee, the local authority will then assess whether the property is suitable for the number of people the landlord wants to rent it to. In most case, the local authority, their agents, will visit a property to assess facilities and also fire precautions. A decision will then be taken to grant a license.

There is a fee for registration, councils set the fee and the ones shown below are indicative of a southern local authority:

- Shared houses-five sharers landlords first house £640
- Subsequent house £590
- Plus £10 each additional occupier over five

Hostels
- 10 occupiers £690
- 20 occupiers £790
- 50 occupiers £1100
- 75 occupiers £1340

In summary, The landlord of a HMO has certain duties under the regulations to his tenants:

Duty to provide information
The manager (this means that whoever is charged with the management of the building) must ensure that:
- His name, address and telephone number are available to each household in the HMO

- These details are also clearly displayed in a prominent position in the HMO.

The manager should maintain a log book to record all events at the property such as:
- Testing of fire alarms
- Testing of fire fighting equipment
- Gas safety certificate
- Electrical report
- Inspection and wants of repair

Duty to take safety measures

The manager must ensure that all means of escape from fire in the property are kept free from obstruction and in good order as should all fire alarms and equipment.

The manager should ensure that the structure is designed and maintained in a safe condition, and also take steps to protect occupiers from injury. In properties with four or more occupants, the Regulations provide that fire escape notices be clearly displayed.

Duty to maintain water supply drainage

The manager must ensure that the water supply and drainage system serving the property are maintained in a good working condition. More specifically, water fittings should be protected from frost and all water storage tanks should be provided with covers.

Duty to supply and maintain gas and electricity

The manager must supply the local housing authority within 7 days of receiving a written request a safety certificate. The manager must ensure that the fixed electrical installation is checked at least once every three years by a suitably qualified electrician and supply this to the LHA on written request.

In addition to the above, there is a duty to maintain common parts, fixtures, fittings and appliances. There is a duty to maintain living accommodation and to provide waste disposal facilities.

Powers of the local authority in relation to HMO's

It is essential to ensure that, if you have invested in a HMO that you manage it rigorously because local authorities have sweeping powers to fine landlords and to revoke licenses. A local authority can prosecute a landlord who does not obtain a license for a HMO.

Safety generally for all landlords-the regulations

The main product safety regulations relevant to the lettings industry are:

Gas safety

The Gas safety (Installation and use) Regulations 1998
The Gas Cooking Appliances (safety) Regulations 1989
Heating Appliances(Fireguard) (safety) Regulations 1991
Gas Appliances(Safety) Regulations 1995

All of the above are based on the fact that the supply of gas and the appliances in a dwelling are safe. A Gas Safety certificate is required to validate this.

Furniture Safety

Furniture and Furnishings (Fire) (Safety) Regulations 1988 and 1993 (as amended). Landlords and lettings agents are included in these regulations. The regulations set high standards for fire resistance for domestic upholstered furniture and other products containing upholstery.

The main provisions are:

- Upholstered articles (i.e. beds, sofas, armchairs etc) must have fire resistant filling material.
- Upholstered articles must have passed a match resistant test or, if of certain kinds (such as cotton or silk) be used with a fire resistant interliner.
- The combination of the cover fabric and the filling material must have passed a cigarette resistance test.

The landlord should inspect property for non-compliant items before letting and replace with compliant items.

Electrical Safety

Electrical Equipment (Safety) Regulations 1994
Plugs and Sockets etc. (Safety) Regulations 1994.
The Electrical Equipment Regulations came into force in January 1995. Both sets of regulations relate to the supply of electrical equipment designed with a working voltage of between 50 and 1000 volts a.c. (or between 75 and 1000 volts d.c.) the regulations cover all the mains voltage household electrical goods including cookers, kettles, toasters, electric blankets, washing machines, immersion heaters etc. The regulations do not apply to items attached to land. This is generally considered to exclude the fixed wiring and built in appliances (e.g. central heating systems) from the regulations.

The availability of grants
Disabled Facilities Grant

The only mandatory grant is the Disabled Facilities Grant, given to those in need, which has been assessed by an Occupational Therapist-the grant has a ceiling. Information of which can be obtained from the local authority. As the name suggests it is for those who are disabled and are n need of works which will make the property accessible and usable for disabled people.

Disabled Facilities Assistance

Disabled Facilities Assistance is in the form of interest free loans, repayable on disposal of the property. To qualify for DFA a person must be at least 18 years old and a freeholder or leaseholder with at least 10 years to expiry of lease and authority to do the work. The maximum amount of assistance is £25,000 or 50% of the equity existing at the time of application. There are a number of other conditions related to the actual works. Details can be obtained from the local authority.

Decent Homes Loans Assistance

This is available to homeowners to enable them to bring their property up to the national Decent Homes Standard. Homes meet Decent Homes standard if they meet a set of criteria which is laid down by the government, such as thermal insulation, overall state of repair etc. Details of the standards can be obtained from the local authority. There are a number of property related criteria and as the money offered is a loan then it will be means tested.

Common Parts Loan/ Common Parts Assistance

This help and assistance is available to owner occupiers (leaseholders) to assist them to meet their liabilities towards the cost of major refurbishment of the common parts of buildings containing their flats, where one or more of the key components of the common parts are old and require replacement or major repair, leading to one or more of the flats becoming 'non-decent' as defined in government guidance. Key components include external walls, roof structure and covering, chimneys etc. Common parts loans are administered by a third party and offered at a subsidised interest rate. They are repayable on disposal of the property. The criteria for Common Part Loans can be obtained from the local authority.

Landlords Major Works Assistance

Local authorities will usually consider assistance to landlords who elect to bring empty properties back into use as accommodation for homeless people. This will involve leasing properties back to the council for a ten-year period. This scheme will depend on the policy of the local authority.

Minor work assistance

Grants are sometimes available to owner-occupiers and tenants for small-scale work for which they have the responsibility. The aim of such grants will be to ensure the person involved achieves the decent homes standard, improves energy efficiency, improves security or to carry out disabled adaptations as an alternative to DFG. Details of these various grants and the criteria attached to them can be obtained from the local authority.

Energy Innovation Grants

These grants are subject to the availability of funding and are related to the policy of the local authority.

Sanitation health and hygiene

Local authorities have a duty to serve an owner with a notice requiring the provision of a WC when a property has insufficient sanitation, sanitation meaning toilet waste disposal. They will also serve notice if it is thought that the existing sanitation is inadequate and is harmful to health or is a nuisance.

Local authorities have similar powers under various Public Health Acts to require owners to put right bad drains and sewers, also food storage facilities and vermin, plus the containing of disease. The Environmental Health Department, if it considers the problem bad enough will serve a notice requiring the landlord to put the defect right. In certain cases the local authority can actually do the work and require the landlord to pay for it. This is called work in default.

****

8

WHAT SHOULD BE PROVIDED UNDER THE TENANCY

Furniture

A landlords decision whether or not to furnish property will depend on the sort of tenant that he is aiming to find. The actual legal distinction between a furnished property and an unfurnished property has faded into insignificance.

If a landlord does let a property as furnished then the following would be the absolute minimum:

- Seating, such as sofa and armchair

- Cabinet or sideboard

- Kitchen tables and chairs

- Cooker and refrigerator

- Bedroom furniture

Even unfurnished lets, however, are expected to come complete with a basic standard of furniture, particularly carpets and kitchen goods. If the landlord does supply electrical equipment then he or she is able to disclaim any repairing responsibility for it, but this must be mentioned in the tenancy agreement.

Insurance

Strictly speaking, there is no duty on either landlord or tenant to insure the property. However, it is highly advisable for the landlord to provide buildings insurance as he/she stands to lose a lot more in the event of fire or other disaster than the tenant. A landlord letting property for a first time would be well advised to consult his/ her insurance company before letting as there are different criteria to observe when a property is let and not to inform the company could invalidate the policy.

At the end of the tenancy

The tenancy agreement will normally spell out the obligations of the tenant at the end of the term. Essentially, the tenant will have an obligation to:

- have kept the interior clean and tidy and in a good state of repair and decoration
- have not caused any damage
- have replaced anything that they have broken
- replace or pay for the repair of anything that they have damaged
- pay for the laundering of the linen
- pay for any other laundering
- put anything that they have moved or removed back to how it was

Sometimes a tenancy agreement will include for the tenants paying for anything that is soiled at their own expense, although sensible wear and tear is allowed for.

The landlord will normally be able to recover any loss from the deposit that the tenant has given on entering the premises. However, sometimes, the tenants will withhold rent for the last month in order to recoup their deposit. This has become more difficult since the introduction of the tenancy deposit schemes, described earlier. It is up to the landlord to negotiate re-imbursement for any damage caused, but this should be within reason. There is a remedy, which can be pursued in the Small Claims court if the tenants refuse to pay but this is rarely successful.

****

9

REGAINING
POSSESSION OF A PROPERTY

....

Fast-track possession

In normal circumstances, the landlord will have served a section 21 notice on the tenant at the start of the tenancy. This brings the tenancy to an end on the day of expiry, i.e. on the day of expiry of the six month period, or 12 month period, whichever is appropriate. It should be noted that if a landlord takes a deposit from the tenant then every deposit must be registered with the appropriate deposit service before the landlord can serve the s21 notice. It should also be noted that if a section 21 notice is served after the end of the fixed term giving two months notice then the notice should be a section 21 (b). This is important as a service of the incorrect notice can delay proceedings.

On expiry of the notice, if it is the landlord's intention to take possession of the property then the tenants should leave. It is worthwhile writing a letter to the tenants one month before expiry reminding them that they should leave.

In the event of the tenant refusing to leave, then the landlord has to then follow a process termed 'fast track possession'. This entails filling in the appropriate forms (N5B) which can be downloaded from Her Majesty's Court Service Website www.justice.gov.uk.

Assuming that a valid section 21 notice has been served on the tenant, the accelerated possession proceedings can begin and the forms completed and lodged with the court dealing with the area where the property is situated.

In order to grant the accelerated possession order the court will require the following:

- The assured shorthold agreement
- The section 21 notice
- Evidence of service of the section 21 notice

The best form of service of the s21 notice is by hand. If the notice has already served then evidence that the tenant has received it will be required.

A copy must also be served on the tenant. This will be done by the court although it might help if the landlord also serves a copy informing the tenant that they are taking proceedings. If the tenant disputes the possession proceedings in any way they will have 14 days to reply to the court. If the case is well founded and the paperwork is in order then there should be no case for defence. Once the accelerated possession order has been granted then this will need to be served on the tenant, giving them 14 days to vacate. In certain circumstances, if the tenant pleads hardship the court can grant extra time to leave, six weeks as opposed to two weeks. If they still do not vacate then an application will need to be made to court for a bailiffs warrant to evict the tenants.

An accelerated possession order remains in force for six years from the date it was granted.

Going to court to end the tenancy

There may come a time when the landlord needs to go to court to regain possession of a property. This will usually arise when the contract has been breached by the tenant, for non-payment of rent or for some other breach such as nuisance or harassment. As we have seen, a tenancy can be brought to an end in a court on one of the grounds for possession. However, as the tenancy will usually be an assured shorthold then it is necessary to consider whether the landlord is in a position to give two months notice and withhold the deposit, as opposed to going to court. The act of withholding the deposit will entail the landlord refusing to authorize the payment to the tenant online. This then brings arbitration into the frame. Deposit schemes have an arbitration system as an integral part of the scheme.

If the landlord decides, for whatever reason, to go to court, then any move to regain the property for breach of agreement will commence in the county court in the area in which the property is. The first steps in ending the tenancy will necessitate the serving of a notice of seeking possession using one of the Grounds for Possession detailed earlier in the book. If the tenancy is protected then 28 days must be given, the notice must be in prescribed form and served on the tenant personally (preferably).

If the tenancy is an assured shorthold, which is more often the case now, then 14 days notice of seeking possession can be used. In all cases the ground to be relied upon must be clearly outlined in the notice. If the case is more complex, then this will entail a particulars of claim being prepared, usually by a solicitor, as opposed to a standard possession form.

A fee is paid when sending the particulars to court, which should be checked with the local county court. The standard form which the landlord uses for routine rent arrears cases is called the N119 and the accompanying summons is called the N5. Both of these forms can be obtained from the court or from www.courtservice.gov. When completed, the forms should be sent in duplicate to the county court and a copy retained for the landlord.

The court will send a copy of the particulars of claim and the summons to the tenant. They will send the landlord a form which gives him a case number and court date to appear, known as the return date.

On the return date, the landlord will arrive at court at least 15 minutes early. He can represent yourself in simple cases but will be advised to use a solicitor for more contentious cases.

If the tenant is present then they will have a chance to defend themselves.

A number of orders are available. However, if you have gone to court on the mandatory ground eight then if the fact is proved then you will get possession immediately. If not, then the judge can grant an order, suspended whilst the tenant finds time to pay.

In a lot of cases, it is more expedient for a landlord to serve notice-requiring possession, if the tenancy has reached the end of the period, and then wait two months before the property is regained. This saves the cost and time of going to court particularly if the ground is one of nuisance or other, which will involve solicitors.

If the landlord regains possession of your property midway through the contractual term then he will have to complete the possession process by use of bailiff, pay a fee and fill in another form, Warrant for Possession of Land.

****

10

PUBLIC SECTOR TENANCIES

Renting from a social housing landlord

Who is a tenant of a social housing landlord?

You are a tenant of a social housing landlord if you are a tenant of:

- a local authority. These are district councils and London borough councils; or
- a housing association; or
- a housing co-operative.

Local authority tenants

If you are a tenant of a local authority you are likely to be a secure tenant or an introductory tenant. In England, from 1 April 2012, local authorities can also grant flexible tenancies.

Housing association and housing co-operative tenants
Tenancy began before 15 January 1989

If you are a housing association or housing co-operative tenant and your tenancy began before 15 January 1989, you will be a secure tenant. For details about the rights a secure tenant has, see below.

Tenancy began on or after 15 January 1989

If you are a housing association or housing co-operative tenant and your tenancy began on or after 15 January 1989, you are likely to be an assured tenant. Some association tenants may be starter tenants for the first 12 to 18 months. A starter tenancy is a type of assured shorthold tenancy.

In England, from 1 April 2012, housing associations can use assured shorthold tenancies for tenancies other than starter tenancies.

Rights of secure tenants

As a secure tenant you have the right to stay in the accommodation unless your landlord can convince the court that there are special reasons to evict you, for example, you have rent arrears, damaged property or broken some other term of the agreement. As well as the right to stay in your home as long as you keep to the terms of the tenancy, you will also have other rights by law: These include the right:

- to have certain repairs carried out by your landlord
- to carry out certain repairs and to do improvements yourself - see under heading Repairs and improvements
- to sublet part of your home with your landlord's permission
- to take in lodgers without your landlord's permission
- to exchange your home with certain other social housing tenants
- if you are a local authority tenant, the right to vote to transfer to another landlord
- to be kept informed about things relating to your tenancy
- to buy your home.

- if you are a housing association tenant whose tenancy started before 15 January 1989, the right to a 'fair rent' - see under heading Fixing and increasing the rent
- for your spouse, civil partner, other partner or in some cases a resident member of your family, to take over the tenancy on your death (the right of 'succession')
- to assign (pass on) the tenancy to a person who has the right of 'succession' to the tenancy. This is sometimes difficult to enforce
- if you are a local authority tenant, to take over the management of the estate with other tenants by setting up a Tenant Management Organisation
- not to be discriminated against because of your disability, gender reassignment, pregnancy and maternity, race, religion or belief, sex or sexual orientation.

You will usually have a written tenancy agreement which may give you more rights than those set out above.

Complaints about secure tenancies

Each social housing landlord must have a clear policy and procedure on dealing with complaints. You should have the opportunity to complain in a range of ways. If after using your landlord's complaints procedure you are still dissatisfied, you can complain to an Ombudsman about certain problems. In England, if you are a local authority tenant this will be the Local Government Ombudsman, and if you are a housing association tenant it will be the Housing Ombudsman. If you have suffered discrimination, you can complain about this to the Ombudsman. In Wales, you can complain to the Public Services Ombudsman for Wales.

Rights of assured tenants

As an assured tenant you have the right to stay in your accommodation unless your landlord can convince the court there are reasons to evict you, for example, that there are rent arrears, damage to the property, or that another of the terms of the agreement has been broken.

As an assured tenant you can enforce your rights, for example, to get repairs done, without worrying about getting evicted. As well as the right to stay in your home as long as you keep to the terms of the tenancy you will also have other rights by law including:-

- the right to have the accommodation kept in a reasonable state of repair
- the right to carry out minor repairs yourself and to receive payment for these from your landlord - see under heading Repairs and improvements
- the right for your spouse, civil partner or other partner to take over the tenancy on your death (the right of 'succession')
- the right not to be treated unfairly by your landlord because of your disability, gender reassignment, pregnancy and maternity, race, religion or belief, sex or sexuality.

You will usually have a written tenancy agreement which may give you more rights than those set out above.

Complaints about assured tenancies

Each housing association must have a clear policy and procedure on dealing with complaints. You should have the opportunity to complain in a range of ways. If after using your landlord's complaints procedure you are still dissatisfied, you can complain in England, to the Housing Ombudsman, or in Wales, to the Public Services Ombudsman for Wales.

Starter tenancies and assured shorthold tenancies

A starter tenancy is the name often used by housing associations to describe an assured shorthold tenancy. Starter tenancies are probationary tenancies which allow a landlord to evict you more easily if you break the terms of your tenancy agreement.

A starter tenancy generally lasts for 12 months, although they can be extended to 18 months. As long as no action has been taken by the landlord to end the tenancy within the starter period, the starter tenant can then become an assured or longer-term assured shorthold tenant in England, or an assured tenant in Wales.

In England, housing associations can use assured shorthold tenancies for tenancies other than starter tenancies. They are likely to last for a fixed term of five years or more, but in some cases will last for two years. These tenancies may also be on 'affordable rent' terms.

In England, if you have an assured shorthold tenancy of a fixed term of two years or more with a housing association landlord, you will generally have similar rights to an assured tenant. However, if you have a fixed term tenancy, you only have the right to stay in your home for the length of the fixed term.

Complaints about starter and assured shorthold tenancies

Each housing association must have a clear policy and procedure on dealing with complaints. You should have the opportunity to complain in a range of ways. If after using your landlord's complaints procedure you are still dissatisfied, you can complain in England, to the Housing Ombudsman, or in Wales, to the Public Services Ombudsman for Wales.

Fixing and increasing the rent
Secure tenants
Local authority tenancies

Rents for local authority tenants are fixed according to the local authority's housing policy and the amount of money they get from central government. You cannot control the amount of rent payable, but may be able to claim housing benefit to help pay it.

Housing association and housing co-operative tenancies which began before 15 January 1989

If you are a housing association or housing co-operative tenant whose tenancy started before 15 January 1989 you are a secure tenant, but your rent is generally a 'fair rent' registered by the Rent Officer. The housing association or co-operative will usually have had the rent registered.

Once a rent has been registered, a new rent cannot usually be considered for the accommodation for two years. The rent can only be increased if:-

- you ask for a new fair rent assessment after two years
- your landlord asks for a new fair rent assessment after one year and nine months, although any new rent would not become effective until the end of two years.

An application for a rent increase can be made earlier, but only if the tenancy has changed drastically or if you and your landlord apply together. If you need help paying the rent you may be able to claim housing benefit.

Assured tenants

Housing association or housing co-operative tenancies which began on or after 15 January 1989

Many housing association tenants whose tenancy started on or after 15 January 1989 are assured tenants. If you are an assured tenant, your rent is the rent you agreed to pay your landlord at the beginning of the tenancy and should be covered in your tenancy agreement. The tenancy agreement should also state when and how the rent can be increased.

In England, most housing associations and housing co-operatives are registered with the Homes and Communities Agency and must follow standards and procedures set down by this regulatory body. They are sometimes known as social landlords. They set rents in accordance with government guidance and tenants have to be given clear information about how their rent and service charges are set and how they can be changed.

You may have the right to apply to a Rent Assessment Committee if you do not agree to a rent increase.

In Wales, housing associations must manage their housing to standards set by the Welsh Government. You must be informed in writing, and in advance about any changes in your rent. You should be given at least 28 days notice of any increase. You may have the right to apply to a Rent Assessment Committee if you do not agree to a rent increase.

If you are a housing association tenant in Wales, there is a leaflet explaining your rights called The Guarantee for Housing Association Residents. You can find this on the Welsh Government website at: www.new.wales.gov.uk.

If you want to apply to a Rent Assessment Committee you should consult an experienced adviser, for example, a Citizens Advice Bureau. If you need help paying the rent you may be able to claim housing benefit. You may also be entitled to other benefits if you are on a low income or you are unemployed.

To work out which other benefits you may be entitled to, you should consult an experienced adviser, for example, a Citizens Advice Bureau.

Affordable rent

Affordable rent is a type of social housing provided in England by social housing landlords.

The rent is called 'affordable' but it is a higher rent than would normally be charged for social housing. The landlord can charge up to 80% of what it would cost if you were renting the property privately. The extra money from affordable rent homes goes towards building more new social housing.

In most cases, tenancies on affordable rent terms are granted by housing associations. Where the landlord is a housing association, the type of tenancy granted is either an assured or an assured shorthold tenancy. In some cases, a local authority may grant a tenancy on affordable rent terms. Where it does, the tenancy type is either a secure or a flexible tenancy.

An affordable rent can be increased once a year. The maximum amount that an affordable rent can be increased by is Retail Price Index (RPI) + 0.5 %.

doing so when you move out. You will not be eligible for this compensation if you buy your home.

Disabled tenants

If you are disabled, you may be able to have alterations carried out to your home. You may first have to get the need for any alterations assessed by the social services department. Alterations could include the installation of a stair lift or hoist or adaptation of a bathroom or toilet.

If you want to get an alteration carried out you should consult an experienced adviser, for example, at a Citizens Advice Bureau.

A disabled tenant may also be able to get a disabled facilities grant to make the home more suitable.

Gas appliances

Your landlord must make sure that any gas appliances in residential premises are safe. They must arrange for safety checks on appliances and fittings to be carried out at least once every twelve months. The inspection must be carried out by someone who is registered with Gas Safety Register. Their website is: www.gassaferegister.co.uk. The landlord must also keep a record of the date of the check, any problems identified and any action taken. As the tenant, you have the right to see this record as long as you give reasonable notice.

If your landlord does not arrange for checks or refuses to allow you to see the record of the check, you could contact the local Health and Safety Executive office.

If you are on benefits or have a low income you may qualify for housing benefit to help pay some or all of the affordable rent.

Repairs and improvements

As a tenant you have the right to have your accommodation kept in a reasonable state of repair. You have also an obligation to look after the accommodation. The tenancy agreement may give more details of both your landlord's and your responsibilities in carrying out repairs and you should check this. We have discussed repairs earlier in the book.

Certain repairs will almost always be your landlord's responsibility, whether or not they are specifically mentioned in the tenancy agreement. These are:-

- the structure and exterior of the premises (such as walls, floors and window frames), and the drains, gutters and external pipes. If the property is a house, the essential means of access to it, such as steps from the street, arc also included in 'structure and exterior'. It also includes garden paths and steps
- the water and gas pipes and electrical wiring (including, for example, taps and sockets)
- the basins, sinks, baths and toilets
- fixed heaters (for example, gas fires) and water heaters but not gas or electric cookers.

The Right to repair

Tenants of local authorities and other social landlords (including housing associations) can use 'right to repair' schemes to claim compensation for repairs which the landlord does not carry out within a set timescale.

Local authority tenants have a right to repair scheme which they must follow. Under the scheme, if repairs are not carried out within a fixed time scale, you can notify your landlord that you want a different contractor to do the job. The local authority must appoint a new contractor and set another time limit. You can then claim compensation if the repair is not carried out within the new time limit.

As a local authority tenant, you can currently use the 'right to repair' scheme for repairs which your landlord estimates would cost up to £250. You can also claim up to £50 compensation. Twenty types of repairs qualify for the scheme, including insecure doors, broken entry phone systems, blocked sinks and leaking roofs.

A repair will not qualify for the scheme if the local authority has fewer than 100 properties, is not responsible for the repair or if the authority decides it would cost more than £250.

If you're the tenant of another social landlord, such as a housing association, you are entitled to compensation if you report a repair or maintenance problem which affects your health, safety or security and your landlord fails twice to make the repair within the set timescale.

There is a flat rate award which is currently £10, plus £2 a day up to a total of £50, for each day the repair remains outstanding. A maximum cost for an eligible repair may be set by the individual landlord.

Improvements

As a local authority tenant if you make certain improvements to your home, for example, loft insulation, draught proofing, new baths, basins and toilets and security measures, you can apply for compensation for

The housing association will then have to obtain a possession order from the county court by proving that one of the 'grounds for possession' applies. We discussed grounds for possession earlier in the book.

Social housing tenancies and discrimination

When renting accommodation from a local authority, housing association or other social landlord, they must not discriminate against you because of your disability, gender reassignment, pregnancy and maternity, race, religion or belief, sex or sexual orientation. This means that they are not allowed to:

- rent a property to you on worse terms than other tenants
- treat you differently from other tenants in the way you are allowed to use facilities such as a laundry or a garden
- evict or harass you because of discrimination
- charge you higher rent than other tenants
- refuse to re-house you because of discrimination
- refuse to carry out repairs to your home because of disrimination
- refuse to make reasonable changes to a property or a term in the tenancy agreement which would allow a disabled person to live there.

If you think your landlord is discriminating against you, you should get advice from an experienced adviser, for example, at a Citizens Advice Bureau.

Introductory tenants -who is an introductory tenant?

Some local authorities make all new tenants introductory tenants for the first 12 months of the tenancy.

Rights of introductory tenants

Introductory tenants have some but not all of the rights of secure tenants. The following table shows your rights as an introductory tenant compared with secure tenants.

Statutory right	Secure tenant	Introductory tenant
Right to succession by partners or in some cases family members	yes	yes
Right to repair	yes	yes
Right to assign	yes	no
Right to buy	yes	no, but period spent as an introductory tenant counts towards the discount
Right to take in lodgers	yes	no
Right to sub-let part of your home	yes	no
Right to do improvements	yes	no
Right to exchange your home with certain other tenants	yes	no
Right to vote prior to transfer to new landlord	yes	no
Right to be consulted on housing management issues	yes	yes
Right to be consulted on decision to delegate housing management	yes	yes
Right to participate in housing management contract monitoring	yes	yes

Ending an introductory tenancy

At the end of the twelve months, provided there have been no possession proceedings against you, the introductory tenancy will usually be converted by your landlord to a secure tenancy. However, your landlord may decide to extend the introductory tenancy for a further six months. If this happens, you will be told the reasons for the decision and given the chance to ask for the decision to be reviewed.

Possession proceedings

It is very easy for a landlord to evict an introductory tenant. If you have received a notice from the landlord stating that they intend to evict you and take possession of the property, you should immediately consult an experienced adviser, for example, at a Citizens Advice Bureau.

Flexible tenants

Flexible tenancies are a type of tenancy that can be granted by local authority landlords in England, from 1 April 2012. Not all local authorities offer them.

A flexible tenancy is similar to a local authority secure tenancy. However, a secure tenancy is periodic, which means that it lasts for an indefinite period of time. Periodic tenancies are often called 'lifetime tenancies'. In contrast, a flexible tenancy lasts for a fixed period of time. In most cases, a flexible tenancy will last for at least five years.

A local authority has to serve a written notice on you before a flexible tenancy can start. The notice must tell you that the tenancy you're being offered is a flexible tenancy, and what the terms of the tenancy are.

Flexible tenants have a number of legal rights, many of which are similar to the rights of secure tenants. For example, the right to pass on your tenancy when you're alive or when you die, the right to exchange your home with certain other tenants, and the right to buy your home.

A local authority doesn't have to grant you another tenancy when the fixed term of the flexible tenancy comes to an end. You can ask the local authority to review its decision not to grant you another tenancy. The review will consider if your landlord has followed its policies and procedures when making that decision.

If you are not given another tenancy when your flexible tenancy comes to an end, the local authority will take action to evict you.

****

11

PRIVATE TENANCIES IN SCOTLAND

The law governing the relationship between private landlords and tenants in Scotland is different to that in England. Since the beginning of 1989, new private sector tenancies in Scotland have been covered by the Housing (Scotland) Act 1988. Following the passage of this Act, private sector tenants no longer have any protection as far as rent levels are concerned and tenants enjoy less security of tenure.

There are four essential elements in the creation of a tenancy under Scottish law:

- An agreement between landlord and tenant
- The payment of rent. If someone is allowed to occupy a property without an agreement then this will not amount to a tenancy
- A fixed permission date (called an 'ish')
- Possession

The agreement must be in writing if the tenancy is for a period of 1 year or more. Agreements of less than a year can be oral.

Protected tenancies

Before 1989, most private sector tenancies were likely to be protected tenancies. A protected tenancy is a contractual tenancy covered by the Rent Act (Scotland) 1984 and must satisfy the following requirements:

- The house must be let as a dwelling house (this can apply to a house or part of a house)
- The house must be a separate dwelling
- The ratable value must be less than a specified sum

Various categories of dwellings did not qualify as protected tenancies. A protected tenancy retains its status until the death of a tenant or his spouse, or any eligible successor, and therefore some protected tenancies are still in existence today.

Grounds for possession

As is the case in England and Wales, where there is no protected tenancy, the landlord may possess a property only by obtaining a court order. The landlord must serve a notice to quit, giving 28 days notice. A ground for possession must be shown, either discretionary or mandatory before possession can be given.

The grounds for possession are similar to those in England and Wales, with ten mandatory and ten discretionary grounds applying.

Fair rent system

A fair rent system, similar to England and Wales, exists in Scotland for protected tenants. There is a set procedure to be followed, with either the landlord or tenant, or jointly, making an application to the rent officer. Once fixed, the rent is valid for three years. A fresh application can be made within three years if circumstances relating to the tenancy radically alter, such as a substantial refurbishment.

Assured tenants

Under the Housing (Scotland) Act 1988, the assured tenancy was introduced into Scotland coming into force after 2nd January 1989. This is very similar indeed to the assured tenancy introduced into England and Wales in 1989. A Scottish assured tenancy has three elements:

- the tenancy must be of a house or flat or self contained dwelling. For an agreement to exist, there must be an agreement, rent payable a termination date and possession, as there is in all leases in Scotland
- The house must be let as a separate dwelling. A tenancy may be of a flat, part of a house, or even a single room, provided it is possible for the tenant to carry on all 'the major activities of residential life there, i.e. sleeping, cooking and feeding.
- The tenant must be an individual. A company cannot be given an assured tenancy

The list of exclusions from assured tenancy status are the same as those in England and all the other provisions concerning rent, sub-letting succession, security of tenure and so on, apply.

The grounds for possession and the law governing termination of tenancies is a reflection of English Law.

Short assured tenancies

The Housing Act (Scotland) also introduced 'short assured tenancies', a distinct form of assured tenancy for a fixed term of six months. Again, this is a reflection of the assured shorthold with the same provisions applying.

12

RELATIONSHIP BREAK DOWN AND HOUSING RIGHTS

When a relationship breaks down, whether the people in question are married or not, problems can often occur in relation to the property that was home. The rights of people will depend mainly on whether they are married or not, whether there are children involved and the legal status of individuals in the home.

Housing rights in an emergency

In the main, it is women who suffer from domestic violence. This section refers to women but the rights are the same for men.

If you are a woman, and have been threatened by a man and are forced to leave your home then there are several possibilities for action in an emergency. The first of these is either going to a women's refuge. These provide shelter, advice and emotional support for women and children. These refuges will always try to admit you and as a result are sometimes crowded. They will always try to find you somewhere to live in the longer term. Refuges have a 24-hour telephone service if you need to find somewhere. For addresses see *useful addresses* at the back of this book.

Approaching the council

A person suffering domestic violence who has been forced to flee can approach the local council and ask for help as a homeless person.

Councils will demand proof of violence and you will need to get evidence from a professional person, such as doctor or social worker or police. The council decides whether or not it has a duty to help you and you should seek advice if they refuse. Some councils, but not all will offer help to battered women. If you are accepted as homeless then the council should not send you back to the area where the violence began.

Obtaining a court order

Another course of action in an emergency is to obtain a court order against the man you live with. Courts can issue orders stating that a man:

- Should not assault you or harass you
- Not to assault any children living with you
- To leave the home and not to return
- To keep a certain distance from your home or any other place where your children go regularly.
- To let you back in your home if you have been excluded.

If you believe a court order would help, you should get advice on where to find a solicitor or law centre that deals with these types of applications to the court. Certain orders are harder to get than others, such as exclusion orders. Matters need to be very serious indeed before such an order will be made. However, you will be advised of this when approaching a solicitor or law centre. Failure to obey the terms and conditions laid down in the order can lead to arrest for contempt and a fine or even imprisonment.

Long term rights to the home

Long term rights to stay in a home depend on a number of circumstances. If you are married and the ownership or tenancy of the property is in joint names you have equal rights to live in the property. If it is owned then you will have a right to a share of the proceeds if it is sold. In certain circumstances you have a right to more (or less) than a half share, or to the tenancy in your name after divorce.

If you are married but the ownership or tenancy is in one name only there are laws to protect the rights of the other party. Courts have the power to decide who has the ownership or rights over the matrimonial home, even if the property is held in one persons name only. This can also apply to people who were married but are now divorced and to those who were planning to get married within three years of their engagement.

Spouses who are not the owner or tenant of the home have a right to stay there. The court has the power to exclude either of the spouses, even if they are sole or joint owner or tenant. If your husband has left and stopped paying the rent or mortgage payments, the landlord or building society is obliged to accept payments from you, if you wish to make them, even if the property is not in your name. If the home is owned by your husband then you can register your right to live in it. This prevents your husband selling the home before the court has decided who should live there. And also prevents him taking out a second mortgage on the property without your knowledge. This is known as 'registering a charge' on the home. The court also has the power to transfer a fully protected private tenancy, an assured tenancy or a council or housing association tenancy from one partner to another.

If the matrimonial home is owner occupied and proceedings have started for a divorce, the court will decide how the value of the property will be divided up. The law recognises that, even if the property is in the husbands name only, the wife has a right to a share in its value, that she often makes a large unpaid contribution through housework or looking after children and that this should be recognised in divorce proceedings.

The court looks at a number of things when reaching a decision:

- The income and resources of both partners
- The needs of you and your husband
- The standard of living that you and your husband had before the marital breakdown
- Ages of partners and length of marriage
- Contributions to the welfare of the family
- Conduct of partners
- Loss of benefits that you might have had if the marriage had not have broken down.

The court also has to consider whether there is any way that they can make a 'clean break' between you and your husband so that there are no further financial ties between you. In certain circumstances, the court can order sale of the matrimonial home and the distribution of proceeds between partners.

If you are not married
If you are not married then your rights will depend on who is the tenant or the owner of the home.

Tenants

If a tenancy is in joint names then you both have equal rights to the home. You can exclude your partner temporarily as we have seen by a court order. If you are a council tenant then you may want to see if you can get the council to rehouse you. You should get advice on this from an independent agency (see useful addresses).

If the tenancy is in your partners name only then the other person can apply for the right to stay there, for their partner to be excluded or for the tenancy to be transferred.

Home owners

If you live in an owner occupied property you and you partner may have certain rights to a share of the property even if you are not married.

If the home is jointly owned then you have a clear right to a share in its value. If one person has contributed more than the other then a court can decide that an equal share is unfair. The court cannot order the transfer of the ownership of property but it can order the sale and distribution of the proceeds.

If the home is in one persons name there is no automatic right to live in the home, even if there are children. However, a solicitor acting on your behalf can argue that by virtue of marriage and contribution you should be allowed to stay there and be entitled to a share.

13

HOUSING ADVICE

General advice

Citizens Advice Bureaus, which are situated throughout the U.⊠., provide advice on all problems, including housing and other matters such as legal, welfare benefits and relationship breakdown. If appropriate they can refer you for more specialist help to a solicitor or advice agency. This advice is free of charge. However, suffice to say CAB's have been the target of the coalition government's ongoing wisdom, with them seeking to reduce grant drastically making it harder for the ordinary citizen to seek advice. To find a local office, look in the telephone directory under National Association of Citizens Advice Bureau.

Housing Advice Centres

In many areas there are specialist advice centres offering housing aid and advice. The service they offer varies from one-off information to detailed help over a long period. There are two main types of housing advice centres, Local council housing aid centres which can advise on all kinds of problems, although they will not be able to take action against their own council. Independent housing aid centres may be better equipped to do this. These centres can offer detailed assistance over a length of time and also one-off advice. There a number of independent housing aid centres throughout the country operated by Shelter. You should contact Shelter for your nearest centre.

Other specialist advice

Law centers-they offer free advice and can sometimes represent you in court. They can usually advise on all aspects of law and also advise battered women. They cannot, however, take divorce cases. For this you will need a solicitor. Shelter can provide a list of law centers.

For advice on welfare rights you should try the local council, who may employ a welfare rights advisor. Advisers can also contact the advice line which is run by the Child Poverty Action Group. For women's rights the Women's Aid Federation England and Welsh Women's Aid refer battered women, with or without children, to refuges. They can put you in touch with sympathetic solicitors and local women's aid groups and can offer a range of other advice, such as welfare benefits.

For immigration advice, the Joint Council for the Welfare of Immigrants offers advice on all types of problems connected with immigration and nationality. The United Kingdom Immigrants Advisory Service offers advice and help on problems with immigration. The Refugee Council has an advice service for refugees and asylum seekers.

Advice from solicitors

Solicitors can advise you on all aspects of the law, represent you in certain courts and, if necessary, get a barrister to represent you. It is best to find a solicitor who specialises in housing rights as they usually have a wider knowledge of specific areas. You can get a list of solicitors who specialise in housing law from the Community Legal Service (CLS) Directory in your local library. The list is also on the CLS website. Citizens Advice Bureaus can also supply specialist solicitor details.

Free advice and help

The Legal Help Scheme, whilst also being squeezed, can pay for up to two hours worth of free advice and assistance and for matrimonial cases up to three hours. The scheme is means tested and you must come within the limits of the scheme to qualify. For details of the scheme you should approach a Citizens Advice Bureau or a solicitors practice operating the scheme. You must have reasonable grounds for defending an action. In certain cases, if you succeed in obtaining cash compensation then you may have to pay a proportion of it back, this is known as the *statutory charge*

****

14

THE LONG TENANT- THE LAW AND LEASEHOLDERS

Freehold and Leasehold

For practical purposes, the strongest form of title to land is that of freeholder. Freehold title lasts forever; it may be bought and sold, or passed by inheritance. In short, freehold title is tantamount to outright ownership, and is taken as such for the purposes of this section. Freeholders may, of course, use their land for their own purposes.

The freehold homeowner is merely the most familiar example. But they may also, if they wish, allow other people to use their land. And this is where leases, and other forms of tenure, come in. A lease grants the leaseholder permission to use the land for a certain period, which can be anything from a day or two to several thousand years. It will usually attach conditions, for example that the leaseholder must pay rent (usually a sum of money, although in principle other goods or services could constitute rent).

The lease may, but does not have to, put certain restrictions on what the leaseholder may do with the land. But it must, in order to be a lease rather than merely a licence, grant the leaseholder 'exclusive possession'. This is the right to exclude other people, especially the landlord, from the land. Such a right need not be absolute, and exceptions to it are explained later in the book: but it is enough to give the leaseholder a high degree of control over the land, which has become, for the duration of the lease, very much the leaseholder's land rather than the freeholder's. A lease may be bought, sold, or inherited; if this happens, all the rights and duties under it pass to the new owner.

Leases and Tenancies

Confusion is often caused by the fact that, although the terms leaseholder (or lessee) and tenant are legally interchangeable, they tend to be used in different senses. The tendency is to refer to short leases as tenancies: the more substantial the rights conferred, and the longer the period for which they run, the likelier it is that the agreement will be referred to as a lease. The position of a leaseholder is very different. The major financial commitment will usually be a substantial initial payment either to the landlord (if the lease is newly created) or to the previous leaseholder. There is still a rent, called a ground rent, payable to the landlord, but it is usually a notional amount (£50 or £100 a year is not uncommon). Its purpose is not so much to give the landlord an income as to give the leaseholder an annual reminder that ultimate ownership of the land is not his.

Most residential leasehold property consists of flats. Of these, most are in the private sector, comprising purpose-built blocks and (especially in London) conversions of what were once large single houses. The freehold will usually belong to the developer, to a property company, or sometimes to the original owner of the site.

Shared ownership

A result of the trend towards home ownership has been the dramatic expansion of shared ownership (or low cost home ownership). This is usually administered by housing associations and, although this form of housing provision has been affected by the downturn people seem to be turning back to it as it doesn't require the usual high up front costs such as a hefty deposit. This is a form of tenure that combines leasing and renting. However, the term 'shared ownership' is something of a misnomer because ownership is not, in fact, shared between the leaseholder and the freeholder. The lease relates to the whole property, not part of it, and the shared owner is as entitled as any other leaseholder to consider himself the owner of his house. The key point about shared ownership leases is not that they give an inferior form of tenure to other leases but that they have different conditions attached. The leaseholder pays less than the full value of the lease; typically, half. In exchange for this concession, he pays not the normal notional ground rent but a much more substantial rent. However, he is much more a leaseholder than he is a tenant, and, like other leaseholders (but unlike tenants) is responsible for the internal repair of the property and, in the case of houses, usually the fabric of the building too.

Shared owners usually have the right to increase their stake as and when they can afford it: this is called 'staircasing' because the owner's share goes up in steps. If the property is a house, the freehold will normally be transferred when the owner's share reaches 100%, and he will then be in the same position as any other freehold home owner. If it is a flat, he will continue to be a leaseholder but there will no longer be a rental (other than ground rent).

Obligations of leaseholders and freeholders
The obligations of both parties is contained within the lease. Consumer legislation can also apply to leases; in particular, the Unfair Terms in Consumer Contracts Regulations 1999 (which replace earlier regulations made in 1995) have a major impact. These apply to standard terms in contracts. This means they normally cover the terms

of leases, which are usually presented to potential leaseholders as a package with no opportunity to renegotiate individual terms. Occasionally, however, individual terms can be specifically negotiated and it should be noted that in that case the Unfair Terms Regulations do not apply. Nor will they apply to any lease granted before the earlier version of the regulations came in, in July 1995. The Office of Fair Trading has issued advice about the types of term that are likely to be judged unfair in the context of assured tenancies. The OFT has not issued advice about long leases, but it is likely that similar standards would apply.

Restrictive clauses in leases

So far, we have looked at leases as if they were consumer contracts, and outlined some of the clauses they may contain that could affect leaseholders in their capacity as consumers. But there are some further potentially difficult terms that relate specifically to property issues. These terms are not necessarily unreasonable. For example, in a lease concerning an upstairs flat it would be quite normal to have a clause requiring the leaseholder to keep the premises carpeted. This makes sense because bare floors, although currently very fashionable, could be very noisy for the people in the flat below.

The Office of Fair Trading's advice identifies several types of sweeping provisions that would, if they were enforced, considerably restrict the tenant's ability to live a normal life. Although the OFT's advice relates to assured tenancies, similar objections would probably apply to these clauses in leases. For example:

- **Pets** Leases often lay down that the leaseholder may not own pets, or may not do so without the freeholder's permission.

108

- **Upkeep** Leases may say that the leaseholder must decorate periodically - say, every five or seven years. Where there is a garden, it is common for the leaseholder to be required to keep it in good order.
- **Business** Leases often lay down that the leaseholder must not run any sort of business from his home.

- **Use as residence** A lease will generally say that the property is to be used for the residential purposes of the leaseholder and his household, and that it cannot be sublet. It will sometimes attempt to restrict how many people may live there apart from the leaseholder.

- **Other** Leases sometimes forbid such things as the keeping of flammable materials and the installation of television aerials or satellite dishes. They may require leaseholders to drain hot water systems whenever they are away, or keep the premises clean and free of dust.

It is easy to see why freeholders want such clauses in the lease: it is because they realise that there will be serious problems if someone attempts, for instance, to keep four alsatians in a studio flat. The neighbours will be inconvenienced and will complain to the freeholder, and leases of other flats in the same block will become difficult to sell. The same arguments could apply if one of the leaseholders allows his flat to fall into complete decorative decay or if he runs a noisy and busy trade from his home.

Restrictions on sale
Some leases restrict the kind of person to whom the lease may be sold

(or 'assigned' - see below). For example, a housing scheme may have been intended specifically for the elderly. Clearly, it will not be maintained as such if leaseholders are free to assign or bequeath their leases to whomever they please, so the lease will say that it may be assigned only to persons above a certain age, and that if it is inherited by anyone outside the age group it must be sold on to someone qualified to hold it. Although this could be described as an onerous term because it makes it more difficult to find a buyer and may reduce the lease's value, it is reasonable given the need to ensure that the scheme continues to house elderly people exclusively. And the restriction it imposes is not too severe because so many potential purchasers qualify. However, some leases define much more narrowly to whom they may be sold.

Sometimes the freeholder is a body owned and run by the leaseholders themselves, and in these cases it is usual to require that all leaseholders must join the organisation and, if they leave it, must immediately dispose of the lease to someone that is willing to join. Again, such a term is not necessarily unacceptable. If the organisation makes relatively light demands on its members (perhaps no more than a modest admission fee or annual subscription), the restriction is unlikely greatly to diminish the value of the lease. If, however, the organisation expects much more from its members - perhaps that they actively take part in running it, or that they pay a large annual subscription - the value of the lease will be severely reduced because it will be difficult to find purchasers willing to accept the conditions. A key point is whether the organisation has power to expel members, thus forcing them to sell; and, if so, in what circumstances can this be done.

Access

Virtually any lease will contain a clause allowing the freeholder to enter the property in order to inspect or repair it. This has the effect of qualifying the leaseholder's right of exclusive possession (see below), but only subject to certain conditions. The freeholder (or the freeholder's servants, such as agents or contractors) may enter only at reasonable times, and subject to the giving of reasonable notice. If these conditions are not met, the leaseholder is under no obligation to allow them in; and, even when the conditions are met, the landlord will be trespassing if he enters the property without the leaseholder's consent. If the leaseholder refuses consent even though the time is reasonable and reasonable notice has been given, the landlord's remedy is to get a court order against the leaseholder compelling him to grant entry. It is probable, in such a case, that the landlord will seek, and get, an award of legal costs against the leaseholder.

Arbitration

Many leases contain clauses providing that disputes can be submitted to arbitration at the request of either party. By the Commonhold and Leasehold Reform Act 2002, the effect of these clauses is limited, because the results will not be binding so far as the Leasehold Valuation Tribunal is concerned. If, however, once a dispute has arisen, the parties to agree to submit it to an agreed arbitrator, they are bound by the result, which is enforceable by the courts. If such a 'post-dispute' arbitration finds that the leaseholder is in breach, this is equivalent to a finding by the LVT and will (if the other requirements are met) allow the freeholder to proceed with forfeiture. Arbitration may be a useful mechanism in some cases, and it may be cheaper and quicker than legal action, but it may be difficult to find an arbitrator in whom both parties have confidence.

111

Obligations of Freeholders

Exclusive possession and quiet enjoyment

The first and most important obligation on the freeholder, without which there would be no legal lease at all, is to respect the leaseholder's rights of 'exclusive possession' and 'quiet enjoyment'..

However, the leaseholder's right to quiet enjoyment applies only to breaches by the freeholder or the freeholder's servants such as agents or contractors. It is important to note this because the term is sometimes thought to mean that the freeholder must protect the leaseholder against any activity by anyone that interferes with his use of the property: this is not so. For example, if the freeholder carries out some activity elsewhere in the building that interferes with the leaseholder, the leaseholder's right to quiet enjoyment has been breached and he is entitled to redress unless the freeholder can show that the activity was necessary, for instance to comply with repairing obligations under the lease. But if the interference is caused by someone else, perhaps another leaseholder, the freeholder's obligation to provide quiet enjoyment has not been breached. And it is worth stressing in this connection that even if the other leaseholder is in breach of his lease, it is entirely up to the freeholder whether or not to take action: other leaseholders have no power to force the freeholder to deal with the situation.

This means that if one leaseholder is breaking his lease by holding noisy parties late at night, the other leaseholders may ask, but may not require, the freeholder to take action to enforce the lease.

They may, however, take legal action directly against the offending leaseholder for nuisance.

The 'section 48' notice

Another important protection for leaseholders is found in section 48 of the Landlord and Tenant Act 1987. This was designed to deal with the situation in which freeholders seek to avoid their responsibilities by (to put it bluntly) doing a disappearing act. Sometimes freeholders would provide no address or telephone number or other means of contact, meaning that leaseholders were unable to hold the freeholder to his side of the agreement. Sections 47 and 48 therefore lay down that the freeholder must formally notify the leaseholder of his name and give an address within England and Wales at which he can be contacted, and that this information must be repeated on every demand for rent or service charge. This has proved especially valuable for leaseholders where the freeholder lives abroad, or is a company based abroad. It should be noted that the address does not have to be the freeholder's home, nor, if the freeholder is a company, its registered office; often it will be the address of a solicitor or property management company, or simply an accommodation address. But the key point is that any notice, or legal writ, is validly served if sent to that address, and the freeholder is not allowed to claim that it never came to his notice.

It is not necessary for the notice required by section 48 to be given in a separate document; it is enough if the name and address is clearly given as part of some other document such as a service charge demand. But if the necessary notice is **not** given, no payment of rent, service charge, or anything else is due to the freeholder; the leaseholder may lawfully withhold it until section 48 is complied with. But leaseholders withholding payments on this ground must be careful; once the notice is given, it has retrospective effect, so that all the money due to the freeholder then becomes due immediately. Any leaseholder withholding money on the grounds that section 48 has not been complied with should, therefore, make sure that he has the money easily available so that he can pay up if he has to.

Good management

The freeholder is under an obligation to ensure that his management responsibilities are carried out in a proper and appropriate way. Leaseholders can challenge the freeholder in court or at the LVT if they believe they can show that they are not receiving the standard of management to which they are entitled. This may be an expensive and lengthy process but it better than the alternative, sometimes resorted to by leaseholders, of withholding rent or service charge. This is risky because, whatever the shortcomings of the freeholder's management, it puts the leaseholders in breach of the conditions of their lease and, as such, demonstrably in the wrong (even if the freeholder may be in the wrong as well).

Withholding due payments is therefore not recommended unless the freeholder is so clearly at fault that arguably no payment is due - for instance, if the service being charged for has clearly not been provided at all (as opposed to being provided inadequately), or if there has been no 'section 48' notice (see above). If leaseholders choose to withhold payment, they are strongly advised to keep the money readily to hand so that they can pay up at once if the freeholder rectifies the problem; the danger otherwise is that they will be taken to court and required to pay immediately to avoid forfeiture (see below).

Powers of Leaseholders over Management

If leaseholders want a scrutiny of the standards of management of their flats, they have power under the Leasehold Reform, Housing and Urban Development Act 1993 to demand a management audit by an

put right. It is also likely that the loser will be obliged to pay the winner's legal costs as well as his own, a penalty often considerably more severe that the requirement to pay compensation.

A much more severe remedy open to the freeholder if the leaseholder is in breach is forfeiture of the lease. This means what it says: the lease is forfeit to the freeholder. Forfeiture is sometimes threatened by the more aggressive class of freeholder but the good news for leaseholders is that in practice courts have shown themselves loath to grant it except in very serious cases. Since the Housing Act 1996 took effect, forfeiture for unpaid service charges has been made more difficult for freeholders; this is covered in the next Chapter.

Where forfeiture is threatened for any reason other than failure to pay rent (which, depending on the terms of the lease, may or may not include the service charge element), the freeholder must first serve a 'section 146 notice', so called after the relevant provision of the Law of Property Act 1925. In this he must state the nature of the breach of the lease, what action is required to put it right; if he wants monetary compensation for the breach, the notice must state this too.

Before the section 146 notice can be issued, it must be established that a breach of the lease has occurred. If the leaseholder has admitted the breach, the notice can be issued; otherwise, it must have been decided by a court, the LVT, or an independent arbitrator that the leaseholder is in breach. Moreover, the breach of the lease specified in the section 146 notice must have occurred during the twelve years preceding the notice. For breaches older than this, no valid section 146 notice can be served and so forfeiture is not available. If the notice is not complied with, the freeholder may proceed to forfeit; but the leaseholder may go to court for relief from forfeiture. In practice, courts have generally been willing to grant relief, but they cannot do so unless it is formally applied for. If the leaseholder, perhaps failing to realise the seriousness of the situation, fails to go to court and seek relief, the forfeiture will go ahead.

If the freeholder breaches the lease, the leaseholder can go to court and seek an order requiring the freeholder to remedy the breach, to pay damages, or to do both. The commonest type of breach complained of by leaseholders is failure to carry out repairs, and this explains why action by leaseholders is less usual; they know that if they force the freeholder to do repairs the costs will be recovered through service charges. Legal action may be the best course if the dispute affects a single leaseholder; but if a number of leaseholders are involved they may well prefer to get rid of the freeholder altogether by collectively enfranchising their leases as described earlier.

Leasehold Valuation Tribunals

Several references have already been made to Leasehold Valuation Tribunals. These bodies operate throughout England and Wales. They are appointed jointly by the Lord Chancellor and (in England) the Environment Secretary and (in Wales) the Welsh Secretary. They perform a large number of quasi-judicial functions in relation to property, especially leasehold property, and feature frequently in this book.

15

LEASEHOLDERS AND SERVICE CHARGES

The Role of Service Charges

By far the commonest cause of dispute between leaseholders and
freeholders is the provision of services and, especially, the levying of
service charges. In extreme cases, leaseholders have been asked to
contribute thousands of pounds towards the cost of major repairs, and
have even suffered forfeiture of the lease if they are unable, or unwilling,
to comply. Happily, such instances are rare; but even where the service
charges are more moderate, they are often resented by leaseholders. The
purpose of this Chapter is to explain the legitimate purpose of service
charges and the legal obligations of both the leaseholder and the
freeholder, and to offer some warnings about the circumstances where
very high service charges are likely to be found.

The difference between long leases and tenancies (short-term and
periodic) was set out earlier. One of its most important consequences is
that services are paid for in a very different way. In a periodic or short-
term tenancy, all the basic costs of providing and managing the housing
are paid out of the rent. It is true that there will sometimes be a service
charge as well, but it normally covers things such as the provision of
heating or communal lighting - things that, however necessary they may
be, are peripheral to the central function of providing housing. As a
result, service charges in rented property are usually quite moderate and
cause little argument.

Contrast the position in leasehold housing. In both types of housing, the landlord is under a legal obligation to the residents to keep the property in good condition and to carry out any work necessary for that purpose; but the landlord of rented property is expected to meet the costs from the rent, whereas the freeholder of leasehold stock has no rent to fall back on (apart from the normally negligible ground rent). How, then, are major costs to be met when they arise? The answer, of course, is from the service charge, which is, therefore, of central importance to the management of leasehold property.

From the freeholder's point of view, the logic of service charges is impeccable. It is perfectly reasonable for freeholders to point out:

- that leaseholders benefit from the work because it has maintained or improved their homes; and
- that the fact that the work has been done means that leaseholders will get a better price when they come to sell; and
- that people that own their homes freehold have to find the money to meet costs of this kind.

To sum up the freeholder's position: the costs have been incurred; the work is for the benefit of the leaseholders; so the leaseholders must pay.

But does this mean that leaseholders have no scope to challenge or query service charges? No; under sections 18 to 30 of the Landlord and Tenant Act 1985, as amended by the 2002 Commonhold and Leasehold Reform Act, they have extensive legal protection against improper or unreasonable charging by freeholders, and this is discussed later in the Chapter. First, however, we should look at how a typical service charge is made up.

The Components of a Service Charge

The lease will say how often service charges are levied: typically, six-monthly or annually. Whereas it was usual to collect ground rent in with the service charge, since the passage of the Commonhold and Leasehold Reform Act 2002, a separate notice must now be issued.

The service charge proper will normally consist of three elements.

- **The management fee** is the charge made by the freeholder, or the freeholder's agent, to cover the administrative cost of providing the service and collecting the charge. Usually it will be much the same amount from one year to the next, but if major works have occurred the management fee will usually be higher to cover the extra costs of appointing and supervising contractors; 15% of the cost of the works is a common figure.

- **Direct costs (routine expenditure)** cover costs such as the supply of electricity to communal areas, building insurance, and the like. Again, these costs are likely to be fairly constant from year to year, so leaseholders know in advance roughly how much they are likely to have to pay.

- **Direct costs (exceptional expenditure)** cover costs that are likely to be irregular but heavy. They usually result from maintenance and repair, and it is because this component of the service charge is so unpredictable that it gives rise to so many problems. Where a house has been divided into leasehold flats, the freeholder's costs will usually be similar to what a normal home owner would be obliged to pay; in other words, the costs may well be in the thousands (for a new roof, say) but are unlikely to be higher. Even so, a charge of £5000 for a new roof, albeit divided between three or four flats, is still a major cost from the point of view of the individual leaseholder, especially if it is unexpected. The situation can be far worse in blocks of flats, where the costs of essential repair and maintenance may run into millions. Replacement of worn-out lifts, for example, is notoriously costly; and costs arising from structural defects are likely to be higher still. Suppose it costs £2 million to remove asbestos from a block of forty flats: the average cost per flat is £50,000, a figure that may well exceed the value of the individual flats, and is likely to be beyond the reach of most leaseholders.

Unreasonable Service Charges
a: *General Principles*
Sections 18 to 30 of the Landlord and Tenant Act 1985, as amended by subsequent legislation, grant substantial protection to leaseholders of residential property. This protection was introduced after complaints of exploitation by unscrupulous leaseholders, who were alleged to be carrying out unnecessary, or even fictitious, repairs at extravagant prices, whilst not providing the information that would have enabled leaseholders to query the bill. The general effect of the Act is to require freeholders to provide leaseholders with full information about service charges and to consult them before expensive works are carried out. It must be stressed, however, that although the Act protects leaseholders against sharp practice by freeholders, and will prevent the recovery of **unreasonable** costs, it will support freeholders, provided they have gone through the necessary formalities described below, in the recovery of their **reasonable** costs, even if those costs are high.

A few leases, namely those granted under the right to buy by local authorities or registered housing associations, have some additional protection under the Housing Act 1985 (see below), but sections 18 to 30 (as amended by the 2002 Commonhold and Leasehold Reform Act) apply to all residential leases where the service charge depends on how much the freeholder spends. They set out the key rules that freeholders must observe in order to recover the cost, including overheads, of 'services, repairs or improvements, maintenance or insurance', as well as the freeholder's costs of management. Sections 18 to 30, as amended, only apply to service charges, not to other charges such as ground rent.

It should be noted that failure by leaseholders to pay the service charge does not relieve the freeholder of the obligation to provide the services. The freeholder's remedy is to sue the leaseholder for the outstanding charges, or even to seek forfeiture of the lease (see below).

Section 19 of the Act provides the key protection to leaseholders by laying down that service charges are recoverable only if they are 'reasonably incurred' and if the services or works are of a reasonable standard.

This means that the charge:
- must relate to some form of service, repair, maintenance, improvement, or insurance that the freeholder is required to provide under the lease;
- must be reasonable (that is, the landlord may not recover costs incurred unnecessarily or extravagantly);
- may cover overheads and management costs only if these too are reasonable.

In addition, the charge must normally be passed on to the leaseholders within 18 months of being incurred, and in some cases the freeholder must consult leaseholders before spending the money. These points are covered below.

The Housing Act 1996 gave leaseholders new powers to refer service charges to the Leasehold Valuation Tribunal (LVT). This is covered below (*Challenging Service Charges*).

b: Consultation with Leaseholders

Section 20 (as amended) provides extra protection where the cost of works is more than a certain limit (£250 per unit).Costs above this level are irrecoverable unless the freeholder has taken steps to inform and consult tenants, following a procedure laid out in the 2002 Act, which states that the landlord must give leaseholders four weeks notice of works, obtain two estimates and then give another four weeks for any objections.

It was mentioned above that there are special cases in which these requirements can be set aside. If a service charge is challenged, it is defence for the freeholder to show that the works were so urgent that there was no time for proper consultation. It is also possible for freeholders to enter into long term agreements to carry out works or provide services over a period of years; if so, they must consult before the agreement is entered into but they need not consult separately before each particular element of expenditure under the agreement. Finally, the LVT has a general power to set aside the usual consultation requirements if it seems fair to do so.

Section 20, as amended by s 154 of the 2002 Act, is important because it gives the leaseholders notification of any unusual items in the offing and gives them an opportunity to raise any concerns and objections. If the leaseholder has any reservations at all, it is vital that they be put before the freeholder at this stage. It is unlikely, in the event of legal action later, that courts or LVTs will support a leaseholder that raised no objection until the bill arrived. It is surprisingly common for freeholders and their agents to fail to comply with the requirements of section 20. This comment applies not only where the freehold is owned by an individual or a relatively small organisation (where mistakes might be more understandable) but also where the freeholder is a large, well resourced body like a local authority (which should be well able to understand and carry out its legal duties).

As a result leaseholders are often paying service charges that are not due, so all leaseholders should, before paying a service charge containing unusual items, ensure that section 20, if it applies, has been scrupulously followed. If not, they can refuse to pay.

c: Other Protection for Leaseholders

Grant-aided works: If the freeholder has received a grant towards the cost of carrying out the works, the amount must be deducted from the service charge levied on leaseholders.

Late charging: Service charge bills may not normally include costs incurred more than eighteen months earlier. The freeholder may, however, notify leaseholders within the eighteen month period that they will have to pay a certain cost, and then bill them later. This may happen if, for instance, the freeholder is in dispute with a contractor about the level of a bill or the standard of work.

Pre-charging: Sometimes a lease will contain a provision allowing the freeholder to make a charge to cover future costs besides those already incurred. This practice, which is perfectly lawful in itself, may be in the interests of the leaseholders by spreading over a longer period the cost of major works. It is, however, subject to the same overall requirement of reasonableness.

Court costs: Section 20C provides protection against a specific abuse of the service charge system by freeholders. Previously, freeholders tended to regard their legal costs as part of the process of managing the housing and thus as recoverable from leaseholders. Such an attitude is not necessarily unreasonable: if, for instance, the freeholder is suing a builder for poor work, he is, in effect, acting on behalf of all the leaseholders and it is fair that they should pay any legal costs. But suppose the freeholder were involved in legal proceedings against one of the leaseholders: if the leaseholder lost, he would probably be ordered to pay the freeholder's costs as well as his own; but if the freeholder lost, and had to pay both his own and the leaseholder's costs, he could simply, under the previous law, recover the money as part of the management element in the service charge. This meant that the freeholder was able to pursue legal action against leaseholders without fear of heavy legal costs in the event of defeat, the very factor that deters most people from too ready a resort to law. To prevent this, section 20C allows leaseholders to seek an order that the freeholder's legal costs must not be counted towards service charges.

Service charges held on trust: Section 42 of the Landlord and Tenant Act 1987 further strengthened the position of leaseholders by laying down that the freeholder, or the freeholder's agent, must hold service charge monies in a suitable interest-bearing trust fund that will ensure that the money is protected and cannot be seized by the freeholder's creditors if the freeholder goes bankrupt or into liquidation. However, public sector freeholders, notably local authorities and registered housing associations, are exempt from this requirement.

Administration charges: These are the freeholder's costs incurred in complying with leaseholders' requests for information and approvals under the terms of the lease. All such charges must be reasonable. Any demand for administration charges must be accompanied by a summary of leaseholders' rights and obligations in relation to them. The LVT has the power to decide whether or not an administration charge is payable, and if so, to whom and by whom together with the amount, date payable and the manner in which it is paid.

Ground rent: Ground rent will be specified in the lease and is usually a fairly modest annual sum in the order of £50 or £100. A separate notice of ground rent must be issued by the landlord.

Insurance: Usually, any insurance required under the lease will be taken out by the freeholder and this is discussed below. Occasionally, however, the leaseholder will be required to take out insurance with a company nominated by the freeholder. If the leaseholder thinks he is getting a poor deal, he can apply to the county court or a Leasehold Valuation Tribunal which, if satisfied that the insurance is unsatisfactory or the premiums are unreasonably high, can order the freeholder to nominate another insurer.

'Period of Grace': When a dwelling is sold under the right to buy by a local authority or non-charitable housing association, the purchaser is given an estimate of service charges for the following five years. This estimate is the maximum recoverable during that time. Some purchasers under the right to buy have, however, had a very rude shock when the five year period of grace expires - see *Exceptionally High Service Charges* below.

d: The role of a recognised tenants' association
The tenants who are liable to pay for the provision of services may, if

they wish, form a recognised tenants' association (RTA) under section 29 of the Landlord and Tenant Act 1985. Note that leaseholders count as tenants for this purpose. If the freeholder refuses to give a notice recognising the RTA, it may apply for recognition to any member of the local Rent Assessment Committee panel ('Rent Assessment Committee' is the official term for a Leasehold Valuation Tribunal when it is carrying out certain functions, not otherwise relevant to leaseholders, under the Rent Act 1977).

An important benefit of having a RTA is that it has the right, at the beginning of the consultation process, to recommend persons or organisations that should be invited to submit estimates. However, the freeholder is under no obligation to accept these recommendations.

Another advantage is that the RTA can, whether the freeholder likes it or not, appoint a qualified surveyor to advise on matters relating to service charges. The surveyor has extensive rights to inspect the freeholder's documentation and take copies, and can enforce these rights in court if necessary.

Against these benefits must be set the principal disadvantage of having a RTA, namely that it weakens the freeholder's obligation to consult individual leaseholders. Where there is a RTA, the freeholder, instead of having to supply copies of the estimates to all leaseholders (or place copies where they are likely to be seen), merely has to send them to the secretary of the RTA, and the individual leaseholders must make do with summaries.

Challenging Service Charges

The Landlord and Tenant Act not only allows leaseholders to take action against unreasonable behaviour by the freeholder; it also enables them to take the initiative. This is done in two ways: by giving leaseholders rights to demand information, and by allowing them to challenge the reasonableness of the charge.

Any demand for service charges must include details about leaseholders' rights and how they can challenge the charges. If this is not done the leaseholder may withhold payment without penalty.

a: Right to information
Freeholders must provide a written summary of costs counting towards the service charge. It must be sent to the leaseholder within six months of the end of the period it covers. The service charge need not be paid until the summary is provided.

The law lays down some minimum requirements for the summary. It must:
- cover all the costs incurred during the twelve months it covers, even if they were included in service charge bills of an earlier or later period (see above for late charging and pre-charging);
- show how the costs incurred by the freeholder are reflected in the service charges paid, or to be paid, by leaseholders;
- say whether it includes any work covered by a grant (see above);
- distinguish: (a) those costs incurred for which the freeholder was not billed during the period; (b) those for which he was billed and did not pay; (c) those for which he paid bills.

If it covers five or more dwellings, the summary must, in addition, be certified by a qualified accountant as being a fair summary, complying with the Act, and supported by appropriate documentation.

The purpose of these rules is to put leaseholders in a position to challenge their service charges. After receiving the summary, the leaseholder has six months in which to ask the freeholder to make facilities available so that he can inspect the documents supporting the summary (bills, receipts, and so on) and take copies or extracts. The freeholder must make the facilities available within 21 days after such a request; the inspection itself must be free, although the freeholder can make a reasonable charge for the copies and extracts. Failure to provide these facilities, like failure to supply the summary, is punishable by a fine of up to £2500.

Very similar rules apply where the lease allows, or requires, the freeholder to take out insurance against certain contingencies, such as major repair, and to recover the premiums through the service charge. This is not unreasonable in itself and will, indeed, often be in the interests of leaseholders. The danger is, however, that the freeholder, knowing that the premiums are, in effect, being paid by someone else, has no incentive to shop around for the best deal. Section 30A of the Landlord and Tenant Act 1985 therefore lays down that leaseholders, or the secretary of the recognised tenants' association if there is one, may ask the freeholder for information about the policy. Failure to supply it, or to make facilities to inspect relevant documents available if requested to do so, is an offence incurring a fine of up to £2500.

It must be acknowledged that the rules allowing leaseholders to require information about service charges are, particularly in view of the £2500 fines, fairly onerous from the freeholder's point of view.

b: Challenging a service charge
Any leaseholder liable to pay a service charge, and for that matter any

freeholder levying one, may refer the charge to a Leasehold Valuation Tribunal to determine its reasonableness. This may be done at any time, even when the service in question is merely a proposal by the freeholder (for instance, for future major works). But the LVT will not consider a service charge if:

-   it has already been approved by a court; or
-   if the leaseholder has agreed to refer it to arbitration; or
-   if the leaseholder has agreed it.

The first of these exceptions is obvious and the second is unlikely to apply very often. The third one is the problem: leaseholders should be careful, in their dealings with freeholders, to say or do nothing that could be taken to imply that they agree with any service charge that is in any way doubtful.

The LVT will consider:
-   whether a service charge is payable and if so when, how, and by whom;
-   whether the freeholder's costs of services, repairs, maintenance, insurance, or management are reasonably incurred;
-   whether the services or works are of a reasonable standard; and
-   whether any payment required in advance is reasonable.

The fees for application to a LVT can be obtained from the LVT and will usually change annually. Appeal against a LVT decision is not to the courts but to the Lands Tribunal.

By section 19 of the Landlord and Tenant Act 1985, any service charge deemed unreasonable by the LVT is irrecoverable by the freeholder.

The determination of service charges by the LVT also plays an important part in the rules governing the use of forfeiture to recover service charges. It is to this that we now turn.

Forfeiture for Unpaid Service Charges

Forfeiture was mentioned at the end of Chapter Two. Briefly, it is the right of the freeholder to resume possession of the property if the leaseholder breaches the lease.

By section 81 of the Housing Act 1996, forfeiture for an unpaid service charge is available to the freeholder only if:

-       the leaseholder has agreed the charge; or
-       the charge has been upheld through post-dispute arbitration or by the Leasehold Valuation Tribunal or a court.

Regarding the first of these, it is necessary only to reiterate the warning to leaseholders to say or do nothing that could possibly be construed as representing their agreement to any service charge about whose legitimacy they have the slightest doubt.

Regarding the second, it should be noted that where the leaseholder has not agreed the service charge, proceedings before the LVT or a court or post-dispute arbitration are necessary before the freeholder can forfeit the lease.

A further requirement is that the amount of money involved must either exceed a certain amount or have been outstanding for a minimum period of time. The Government will set these limits by order. It is currently proposed that the minimum amount will be £350 and the minimum period three years, but this is yet to be confirmed. Note that it is necessary for only one of the requirements to be satisfied.

To sum up, before the freeholder can forfeit:
-    it must have been formally decided that the service charge is due,
-    the amount must exceed the minimum amount or have been owed for the minimum time, and
-    a section 146 notice must have been served (but this requirement does not apply if the service charge is reserved as rent).

****

16

ENFRANCHISEMENT AND EXTENSION OF LEASES

LEASEHOLD REFORM, HOUSING AND URBAN DEVELOPMENT ACT 1993

The area of leasehold enfranchisement has attracted a plethora of media and academic interest since its formal introduction in 1967 and has been amended and expanded over the past four decades. The right of long leaseholders to buy their landlord's interest outright or acquire an extended lease term, is unique to England and Wales and, perhaps unsurprisingly, has led to a number of legal challenges over the years. Landlords and tenants alike are anxious to protect their respective property interests in a market that shows no sign of abating. Consequently, this area of the law is continually evolving.

In general terms, the legislation confers two distinct rights: to purchase the freehold, either individually in relation to leasehold houses, or collectively for a block of flats, or to seek a lease extension. Although these rights are curtailed by the statutory tests for qualification, changes to the legislation, introduced by the Commonhold and Leasehold Reform Act 2002, have made it easier than ever for leaseholders to make a claim.

The requirement that leaseholders must have occupied the property in question for a period of two years (the so-called residence requirement) has largely been swept away and replaced by a new, two year ownership test. Indeed, in the case of a collective enfranchisement, even the ownership requirement has been removed. Likewise, qualification tests based on the property's ratable values and rent have gone, with the result that higher value houses, for example, may now enfranchise.

The Collective Right to enfranchise
What is it?

This gives the right for tenants of flats acting together to purchase the freehold and any headleases of their building. In order for the building to qualify under the Act, it must:
• be an independent building or be a part of a building which is capable of independent development; and
• contain two or more flats held by qualifying tenants; and
• have at least two thirds of the flats held by qualifying tenants.
In order to be a qualifying tenant you must have a long lease which means a lease which, when originally granted, was for a term of more than 21 years. However, you must not own three or more flats in the building. You cannot be a qualifying tenant if you hold a business lease.

Notwithstanding the above, the building will not qualify if:
• it comprises four or less units and has a "resident freeholder";
• more than 25% of the internal floor space (excluding common parts) is used for non-residential purposes;
• the building is part of an operational railway.

How do I prepare for a claim?

Any qualifying tenant can give a notice to his landlord or the managing agent requiring details of the various legal interests in the block. This notice places no commitment on the tenant but the response to the notice should provide the tenant with the information necessary for

There are circumstances where the freeholder can resist a claim on the ground of redevelopment.

If the claim is admitted, then the counter-notice must state, amongst other things:

• which of the proposals contained in the initial notice are acceptable;
• which of the proposals contained in the initial notice are not acceptable and what are the freeholder's counter-proposals –particularly on price;
• whether the freeholder wants a leaseback on any units in the building not held by a qualifying tenant (for example, a flat subject to a short term tenancy or a commercial unit).
• compensation for loss in value of other property owned by the freeholder, including development value consequent to sale

Disputes

If any terms of acquisition (including the price) remain in dispute after two months following the date of the counter-notice, then either party can apply to the leasehold valuation tribunal for the matter in dispute to be determined. This application must be made within six months following the date of the counter-notice or the claim is lost. Most claims are settled by negotiation. If a leasehold valuation tribunal is required to make a determination, then there is a right to appeal that decision to the Lands Tribunal if permission is given to do so.

Completion

Once the terms of acquisition have been agreed or determined by the leasehold valuation tribunal, then the matter reverts to a conveyancing transaction with the parties entering into a sale contract on the terms agreed or determined and thence to completion.

If the matter proceeds to completion, then the participating tenants, through their nominee purchaser, will become the freeholder of the building, subject to the various flat leases. In effect, the participating tenants will replace the existing freeholder. This will put them in a position to grant themselves extended leases.

There may be taxation consequences on granting an extended lease, particularly for second home owners. There will also be responsibilities. The participating tenants will become responsible for the management of the building and the administration of the service charge account in accordance with the covenants in the original leases.

If the nominee purchaser is a company, all participators will be shareholders and some will be officers of that company. These are all matters on which clear professional advice will be needed. It is important to note that an individual tenant has no right to become a participating tenant – even if he is a qualifying tenant. It is a matter for the tenants to resolve between themselves. You can always ask to be allowed to join in, but you will have no remedy if refused. If a group does form without you – and does not need you – you may well find yourself left out.

However, if you are left out, that need not necessarily be the end of the road. This is because of the second major innovation that was introduced by the 1993 Act – the individual right to acquire a new lease.

The individual right to extend leases
What is it?

The individual right to a statutory lease extension applies to all qualifying tenants of flats. The condition is that you must be the tenant of a flat which you hold on a long lease (i.e. a lease for an original term in excess of 21 years). Furthermore, you must have owned the lease for at least two years before the date of the claim. For the purpose of the lease extension, There is no limit to the number of flats you may own in the building and you may extend any or all of them provided that the conditions are met. However, you cannot be a qualifying tenant if you hold a business lease.

Prior to the 2002 Act, the personal representatives of a deceased tenant had no rights to make a claim, even where the deceased tenant was able to fulfill the qualifying conditions. However, such personal Representatives can now make a claim provided that the right is exercised within a period of two years from the date of grant of probate.

What do I get?

If you qualify, then you will be entitled to acquire a new extended lease in substitution for your existing lease. This extended lease will be for a term expiring 90 years after the end of the current lease and will reserve a peppercorn rent throughout the term.

Broadly, the lease will otherwise be on the same terms as the existing lease but the landlord will have certain additional redevelopment rights, exercisable within 12 months before the expiration of the current lease term and within 5 years before the expiration of the extended lease.

The price
The price to be paid for the new lease will be the aggregate of:

- the diminution in value of the landlord's interest in the flat, consequent on the grant of the extended lease; being the capitalised value of the landlord's ground rent and the value of his reversion (being the present near-freehold vacant possession value deferred for the unexpired lease term);
- 50% of the marriage value (the additional value released by the tenant's ability to merge the extended lease with the existing lease) must be paid to the landlord although the marriage value will be deemed to be nil if the existing lease has an unexpired term of more than 80 years at the date of the claim;
- compensation for loss in value of other property owned by the freeholder, including development value, consequent on the grant of the new lease
.

The valuation date is the date of the claim notice. In addition to the price and the tenant's own legal costs and valuation fees, you will also be required to reimburse the freeholder his legal costs and valuation fees.

How do I claim?
The procedure to be followed is very similar to that for collective enfranchisement. It is therefore important to be aware that most of the time limits imposed on the procedural stages of the claim are strict and a failure to do something within the required time frame can have dire consequences for the defaulter.

The qualifying tenant can serve a preliminary notice to obtain information. Thereafter, he serves his notice of claim (in this case called the tenant's notice of claim) which amongst other things needs to state:

• a description of the flat – but not necessarily with a plan;
• sufficient particulars to establish that the lease qualifies;
• the premium being offered – it must be a bona fide offer;
• the terms of the new lease;
• the date by which the landlord must give the counter-notice, being a date not less than two months from the date of service of the tenant's notice.

The landlord is likely to respond with a procedural notice requiring payment of a deposit (equal to 10% of the premium being offered) and asking the tenant to deduce title. The landlord's valuer is also likely to inspect the flat for the purpose of carrying out a valuation.

Within the period specified in the tenant's notice, the landlord must serve his counter-notice. First and foremost, this must state whether or not the claim is admitted. If it is not, then the tenant must decide if he wishes to dispute the rejection through the courts. However, unlike a collective enfranchisement claim where the nominee purchaser makes the application to the court in these circumstances, in the case of the statutory lease extension, it is the landlord who makes the application if he has refused the claim.

Enfranchisement

There are circumstances where the landlord can resist a claim on the ground of redevelopment. If the claim is admitted, then the counter-notice must state, amongst other things:

• which of the proposals contained in the tenant's notice are acceptable;
• which of the proposals contained in the tenant's notice are not acceptable and what are the landlord's counter-proposals – particularly the premium.

Disputes

If either the terms of the lease or the premium remain in dispute after two months following the date of the counter-notice, then either party can apply to the leasehold valuation tribunal for the matter in dispute to be determined.

This application must be made within six months following the date of the counter-notice or the claim is lost. Most claims are settled by negotiation. If a leasehold valuation tribunal is required to make a determination, then there is a right to appeal that decision to the Lands Tribunal if permission is given to do so

Completion

Once the terms of the lease and the premium have been agreed or determined by the leasehold valuation tribunal, then the matter reverts to a conveyancing transaction with the parties proceeding to completion of the new lease.

The tenant can withdraw at any time and there are provisions for the tenant's notice to be considered withdrawn if certain strict time limits are not met by the tenant. As in collective enfranchisement, the tenant is on risk as to costs as from the date of his tenant's notice so it is essential to be prepared and to be properly advised before starting down the road to an extension.

GLOSSARY
A SUMMARY OF IMPORTANT TERMS

FREEHOLDER: Someone who owns their property outright.

LEASEHOLDER: Someone who has been granted permission to live on someone else's land for a fixed term.

TENANCY: One form of lease, the most common types of which are fixed-term or periodic.

LANDLORD: A person who owns the property in which the tenant lives.

LICENCE: A licence is an agreement entered Into whereby the landlord is merely giving you permission to occupy his/her property for a limited period of time.

TRESPASSER: Someone who has no right through an agreement to live in a property.

PROTECTED TENANT: In the main, subject to certain exclusions, someone whose tenancy began before 15th January 1989.

ASSURED TENANT: In the main, subject to certain exclusions, someone whose tenancy began after 15th January 1989.

NOTICE TO QUIT: A legal document giving the protected tenant twenty eight days notice that the landlord intends to apply for possession of the property to the County Court.

GROUND FOR POSSESSION: One of the stated reasons for which the landlord can apply for possession of the property.

MANDATORY GROUND: Where the judge must give possession of the property.

DISCRETIONARY GROUND: Where the judge may or may not give possession, depending on his own opinion.

STUDENT LETTING: A tenancy granted by a specified educational institution.

HOLIDAY LETTING: A dwelling used for holiday purposes only.

ASSURED SHORTHOLD TENANCY: A fixed-term post-1989 tenancy.

PAYMENT OF RENT: Where you pay a regular sum of money in return for permission to occupy a property or land for a specified period of time.

FAIR RENT: A rent set by the Rent Officer every two years for most pre-1989 tenancies and which is lower than a market rent.

MARKET RENT: A rent deemed to be comparable with other non-fair rents in the area.

RENT ASSESSMENT COMMITTEE: A committee set up to review rents set by either the Rent Officer or the landlord.

PREMIUM: A sum of money charged for permission to live in a property.

DEPOSIT: A sum of money held against the possibility of damage to property.

QUIET ENJOYMENT: The right to live peacefully in your own Home.

REPAIRS: Work required to keep a property in good order.

IMPROVEMENTS: Alterations to a property.

LEGAL AID: Help with your legal costs, which is dependent on income.

HOUSING BENEFIT: Financial help with rent, which is dependent on income.

HOUSING ADVICE CENTRE: A center which exists to give advice on housing-related matters and which is usually local authority-funded.

LAW CENTRE: A center, which exists for the purpose of assisting the public with legal advice.

Appendix 1 – Useful addresses

Age UK
Tavis House
1-6 Tavistock Square
London WC1 9NA
0800 169 6565
www.ageuk.org.uk

Child Poverty Action Group
94 White Lion Street
London N1 9PF
020 7837 7979

Equality and Human Rights Commission
0808 800 0082
www.equality-humanrights.com

Consumers Association
2 Marylebone Road
London NW1 4DF
01992 822 800
www.which.co.uk

Disability Alliance
Universal House
88-94 Wentworth Street
London E1 7SA
020 7247 8759